From Bad to Worse

From Bad to Worse

Dawn Walton

ISBN : 1-4196-3329-5
Library of Congress Control Number : 2006902977

To order additional copies, please contact us.
BookSurge, LLC
www.booksurge.com
1-866-308-6235
orders@booksurge.com

From Bad to Worse

Contents

Introduction

How it all began...

I ended up in a Contact Centre accidentally. But then, that's not news to anyone, is it? Who ends up in a Contact Centre on purpose, after all? So how did my journey start? Well I was a developer, programming—nothing but a computer to have conversations with, every day, all day. I only applied for the job in the first place because the job advert said, "Must like cats," and I figured that a programming job with an advert like that was just for me.

It would not have been my choice normally. I always had an angling to work with people, but did not realise how strong this was. So straight out of University my only option was to give up my life to sitting and talking to a computer all day.

Of course, that was never going to work long-term—the cats just weren't enough to keep me there. After all, I could have cats at home!

So I quit the job and headed off into the big wide world, looking for a new job that involved computers and people—and bingo, along came Call Centres.

In some ways I was not typical here. Most people who are currently working in a Contact Centre ended up there by accident. They either:

a)   Were backpacking around the world and needed some money to be able to continue;

b)   Left a particular industry and struggled to get a job so took an agent job as a filler; or

c)   Were in an industry which had a small Contact Centre as part of the main operations, and they suddenly found themselves in charge of a whole Contact Centre business.

These stories are not necessarily unique to the Contact Centre industry. Alternative "filler" options include grape or strawberry picking and putting packages together in fulfilment centres. What is unique in the contact centre industry is that once in, people seldom leave! Ask any room full of people in a contact centre if they chose it as a career and almost nobody will say "yes."

So what we have here is a recipe for disaster—an industry filled with people who never planned to be there—and therefore never trained to be there.

Once in—my story is little different from those of many other people. I had no training, of course. My technical skills were tested, but I was talking to customers and trying my best to get them to solve their own problems—using all my inherent skills—because I knew far less than they did. We were unusual in that our client measured customer satisfaction, but no one looked after our quality or efficiency.

Given that we are all here accidentally, our starting point is bad—the question has to be, how do we get worse?

My first management experience was as a Training Manager. I was the first Training Manager in my company. The role was created as the company grew, and as the only trainer I naturally flowed into the manager role.

One of the key learning moments I experienced was when we gained a new COO. One of the first things he organised was a weekly meeting with the management team. This was the first time I had attended anything this structured. Sounds like a kind of obvious thing to do—but one of the things you learn quickly is that those techniques used in other industries rarely cross over to Contact Centres.

So here I am in my first management meeting ever. The new guy turns to his Contact Centre manager and asks a simple question:

"What was your service level yesterday?"
Quiet.
"Well?"
"I don't know."
"How can you not know?"
"I'll tell you tomorrow."
You can imagine the look on the COO's face.
"So how many people do you have absent today?"
Quiet.
"Well?" (Slightly less patient now.)
"I don't know, I'll tell you tomorrow." (Face now red.)
"Okay, how many seats do we have occupied?" (This should be easy to answer because it does not change too often)
(Scrabbling around with bits of paper.)
Quiet.
"Well?"
"I don't know."

You can see where this was going—nothing good was coming out of it. We now have one very embarrassed and defensive Contact Centre manager and a new COO who has managed to get very frustrated in the management meeting. The rest of us are now looking at each other and reviewing where we are sitting at the table to establish who is next for a kicking! This is how I was introduced to the concepts of managing performance in our industry. This was in 1997. The industry was very new, and our new COO came across from another industry. Nobody was looking at their business in this way, but they were beginning to realise they needed to.

I spent a year on the phones, handling calls from customers day in, day out. We went through a fairly rigorous recruitment process but did not really get any training. When I first started taking calls, I had to write my name and the greeting on a piece of paper in front of me—I was so nervous! This lack of training is what motivated me to take up a training role—after a year I had a pretty good idea of what you needed to know, and also the things that really worked to make a customer happy. At this stage, I had a gut feeling about what made good customer service—but I knew others who did not. This is how you realise that both training an agent and listening to the calls on an ongoing basis is critical.

After a couple of years of first being an agent and then training agents, I realised that I liked this industry and I wanted to get more heavily involved in the bread and butter of the contact centre operations. Although I enjoyed the training role, I was getting increasingly frustrated being sidelined when some form of operational crisis hit the centre. I was fortunate in that the value of training was appreciated in the organisation, but this was not enough for me.

When I approached my manager and expressed this frustration, he suggested that I take on the implementation of a quality standard, called COPC® (Customer Operations Performance Centre Inc.), which the US side of our operations had adopted. Knowing absolutely nothing about quality, I accepted and headed over to Dublin to implement it in a centre we had over there. With hindsight, trying to implement massive change via this programme in a country that was not my home country i.e. they had a different culture—was a recipe for pain! But in this case ignorance was bliss and I attacked the project head-on. I learnt as I went along, and clearly wasted the first 6 months of effort by floundering in various directions with no real clue of where I was heading.

Just short of 2 years later we achieved the COPC® certification, the first company outside of the United States to achieve this, and I was working for a company that was transformed. Staff attrition, absenteeism and satisfaction had all improved, margin had improved and customer and client satisfaction had improved. The site went from being the "bottom of the tree" to a showcase for how to operate.

Once momentum was going, we just kept on rolling with it, heading back to the UK and certifying a site there. As the organisation grew, and gained sites across Europe, we had a framework we could operate with to bring all the sites up to a reasonable level of performance, and we were able to certify locations in the UK, Germany, France and the Netherlands. We also kept our Irish site certified—something that was necessary every year. We had found a formula for driving change and establishing performance thresholds across all the sites we took on.

Then I decided it was time to put my money where my mouth was. I had spent so long telling everyone how to do their jobs, I decided the time had come to prove I could do it. I then took on a 500-seat contact centre with 13 clients that was open from 8 am until 11 pm and supported multiple languages—talk about in at the deep end! However, within 18 months I had reduced absenteeism from double figures to between 3 and 4%. We had reduced attrition from close to 200% to 70%, at the same time we had worked on driving up customer satisfaction and client satisfaction and increased the margin by 2%. So it could be done.

In later years, I was able to build on the approach we had established through the COPC® framework and create a framework specific to the company. This meant that we did not just deliver to an external standard, but we also had our own way of doing things that allowed us to guarantee our clients a consistent, high-performance service irrespective of where that business was placed.

So this is how I know what works and what doesn't. I have had the benefit of trying it all and making the mistakes. Here I am writing this book, allowing you to share in the benefits of learning from my mistakes!

Why this book...

In this book we will explore how to run an effective Contact Centre business by focussing on the common mistakes made and looking at a business model for avoiding them. We will explain how to drive a business from bad to worse in the hope that we can show how to really drive it from good to great This book is written specifically for the Contact Centre industry; however, some of the core concepts we will be exploring apply to any business. This book has been inspired by *Good to Great,* by Jim Collins, in which he examines a series of companies that have moved from being merely good to being sustainably great. In this book, we will begin in a different way. Instead of looking at what makes a company great, we examine what will prevent it from becoming great and then provide you with some techniques to avoid making these mistakes

Chapter 1

What mistakes to make to drive your business from bad to worse

Okay, so let's look at some of the common mistakes we can make if we want to get from Bad to Worse. Don't worry too much if they all feel very relevant to you; you are definitely not alone here. As we go through the book, we will gradually build a picture of how these common mistakes can be avoided. As we go through the book we will refer to the business owner, who may also be called the client. This is the organisation that commissions the contact centre to exist. So on to the mistakes...

Mistake Number 1 - Only do what your client asks

Tricky one, isn't it? But this is the root of all evil. Take this scenario:

1. You need business.
2. Your contact centre has a number of very visible empty seats
3. It's that time of year again—you know the one—when the managers are looking for loose change under the sofa to see if they can scrape up enough to make payroll!
4. You get a chance at a big-name client and you will do anything to win the business.
5. They ask for a bunch of stuff to be tracked and you Figure that you must be able to do it. You will work out how nearer the time.

6.   They think they know Contact Centres, so rather than let you know what experience they want their customers to receive, they tell you what service level, what abandon rate, what AHT, how many weeks training to give your agents and what colour wallpaper to use!

7.   You ask them to provide you with data from their own operation (maybe), but they can't.

This is a scenario that should be familiar to anyone who has been in this business for a while. Its obvious now, isn't it? There is no way you can deliver what they want. It is doomed to failure—preceded by many months of pain for you and your site and a seriously bitter taste left in the mouth for both you and your client.

Mistake Number 2 - Grab the nearest person who walks past the centre and stick a headset on them

We've all done it. These days recruitment is more of a fine art. This was not necessarily the case in the past. The challenge in contact centres is unique. What you need is high volume and high flexibility for what is basically a commodity role. You also need highly skilled individuals who are able to communicate well over the phone, multi-task by logging everything they do into a system, and maintain an acceptable and accurate knowledge of a product line that changes constantly—but you can't pay enough to acknowledge that, because you are in a commodity market. Now, this is a really easy mistake to make on our list of ways to drive our centres from bad to worse! What we end up doing is recruiting for anyone we can get hold of. The aim becomes to have warm bodies sit on the seats, and this is where all the pressure comes from. We may need to interview 100 people to get 15-20 successful candidates. When you have the pressure of volume weighing on you, then surely it must be better to have someone there than no one. Mustn't it?

Of course, when sitting down thinking about this, it is perfectly obvious that we will give ourselves problems down the line—but the reality of most organisations is that whilst quality is talked about and documented as a requirement, the training department is often not treated as a key member of the implementation team, and as such the very valid input they usually have is not considered. Then, when the phone operators are underperforming, it is the guys in training who are blamed for poor or insufficient quality.

Mistake Number 3—Forget the Customer

This is easy to do. None of our roles would exist without the customer—and this includes the whole client business. Why is it, then, when an organisation reviews its performance, customer satisfaction is lowest on the list and margin and service level are highest? A mature organisation makes its customer the first thing to focus on—driving escalations and action off the basis of customer satisfaction results as opposed to finance or efficiency results. Look at your performance dashboards—or whatever it is that you use to measure the performance of your business. Now, how many of the metrics you review measure customer satisfaction in any way? (Not service level, not margin, actual satisfaction). If you do have it on your dashboard at all, how large is the sample size, how often do you review performance? Do you know how it breaks down into the different attributes of satisfaction? When you look into this data you are likely to find a number of things:

1. You look at 20 measures and only 1 of them is customer satisfaction.
2. You look only at the overall satisfaction.
3. Your sample size is tiny in comparison to the sample size of all your other data.
4. You make excuses for not taking action based on an unpredictable trend or circumstances outside of your control.
5. You have no idea what the dissatisfaction level is, only the satisfaction level.

6.   You do not look at what the main call drivers are when you analyse your call volume — or, if you do, it is based on the anecdotal input of your Contact Centre manager.

Mistake Number 4 — Don't check to be sure someone gets it before you let them talk to your customers

So let's assume you do not make mistake number 2 on the list. Let me tell you a story from my own experience as a training manager. We once had a guy in a training class. He was a nice guy. He participated, and worked hard. The only problem was that he was kind of hard to understand. This is obviously a catch in our environment. The problem was, he worked so hard, and when we tried to bring up his communication problem with him, he looked like a puppy we were just about to kick. So we worked it through with him and gave him extra coaching, and eventually he went live on the phones with everyone else.

We did not do any structured call monitoring at that stage. The managers would occasionally dial in to listen to a call. So here I am, sitting in my office, dialling into the call having decided to see how he is coming along. I had missed the very start of the call, but unfortunately came in on the call at the point our "willing" agent was telling the customer off for not listening to him. The customer was getting more and more frustrated as they tried to do what they were told. The agent reached a point where he was saying to the customer, "If you do not listen to me I will terminate this call." Clearly, the customer was stunned by this and asked the agent what exactly he wanted her to do. Of course, it just went downhill from this point, with the agent eventually hanging up on the customer! I ran to the supervisor and gave him a full brief on what had happened. Within a day we had dismissed the agent. The lesson here was that we knew all along he would probably be a problem, but because we did not test or measure this, we went against our better judgement and let him actually interact with our customers. Can you imagine what that customer thought of the client and how much damage that one call did? What about all the other calls we did not catch?

Mistake Number 5 — Ignore your unique edge and added value

Ask yourself what you do well as an organisation. Scrap the first answer that pops up, which is the standard line delivered by the sales team. Then scrap all the stuff that pops up where you don't do things well. What are you left with? Why would someone use your company? Now, have you told anyone this?

If you are an outsourcer, why on earth would a client hand over such an important part of its customer interactions to you? These are the customers who make the client successful or unsuccessful as a business. Now, here you are, a total stranger, saying, "give them to me, I will look after them, trust me."

Why should they not just look after the customers on their own — hire a really good operational person to run their contact centre and not hand anything over and not lose that very important lifeline? You see, your sales force will offer to look after the customers, to add value instead of just handle contacts. Your operational team will consider that handling the contacts *is* adding value! So we have a disconnect, and then we are surprised when our client is not very satisfied at our operational reviews when we tell them what a great job we have done of hitting service level.

Mistake Number 6 — Trust people — Assume too much!

This is an interesting industry. We have no product. No box that we can make smaller, more solid, shinier or a different colour. All we have is the people. But people will do, at best, what they are asked to do, and everyone wants to do things their own way; to make their mark. So when we assume that something is being done as expected, this is where the problems start. Again, ask yourself: Do you really think that the people managing your business are doing the little things like comprehensive performance appraisals with their staff? Remember, paperwork alone does not mean an appraisal has been done as you intended. It is very telling when you speak to an agent who says they have never had an appraisal, and yet when you look in their records there is a neatly typed appraisal record. The key is to look at performance indicators in all areas right to the agent level—the appraisal then draws in these measures and combines them with a development plan to ensure they feel they have somewhere to go!

Mistake Number 7—If the finances are right, you have nothing to worry about. Right?

I was once talking to one of our managers about how her business was going. When asked the question, she put a big smile on her face and answered "great, we are hitting and exceeding our budgeted margin." For most of us this would be the end of the conversation. We could walk away, happy that a good job was being done. However, if you asked why, you would hear that we were getting a fixed management fee from the client that we were not using at the time, so it was pure profit. If you dug even further (as I enjoy doing!) you would learn that our handle times were longer than target, service level was heading in the wrong direction and missing target, and customer dissatisfaction was trending upwards. My response was, "So, basically, it's okay that we are screwing the customers because the money is looking good?"

The reality is that most businesses will focus on those areas that are not hitting obvious performance metrics—often financial. No one glances twice at those areas that are doing well. In reality, what we should ask is not, "What went wrong here?" but "Why is it going right here?"

Mistake Number 8 — Regard the Contact Centre industry as something fundamentally different! Accept different standards

I was once staying in a high grade resort in the Caribbean where the management held a special dinner for returning guests once a week. The resort was all-inclusive, but they put on a special set menu, shut one of the restaurants and sat a manager at each table with the guests so they could find out how each guest's visit was. This was very impressive, and demonstrated a company that really understands the value of word of mouth and repeat business. Acknowledging loyalty is a great way of driving loyalty. All this said, that is not the real point of this little story.

On this particular evening, I ended up at the table with the resort manager I grilled him thoroughly on how he managed the business (much to the annoyance of my husband, who ended up talking to another couple at our table about all the cruises they had taken!). What came to light was that this guy was their "troubleshooting" manager, who spent time in different resorts sorting them out, and also lectured in various locations on hotel and resort management.

I was particularly interested in how he trained the staff of the resort. In the previous resort (run by the same company) I had visited, in Jamaica and not Antigua as in this case, I was amazed at the friendliness and customer service mentality of the staff. As you passed the cleaners in the morning they would ask you if you were having a nice holiday and if you would be returning. The manager told me that it is commonplace in this industry to show someone how to do something up to 20 times before you expect them to be competent. How many calls or contacts of your agents do you observe before you regard them as competent to deal with customers on their own? If your answer gets as high as 5 I will be amazed!

Mistake Number 9 — Use technology to solve the process issues

How many times have you seen it happen? You are getting a new system. You have all the promises of how much better it is going to make life than the older system because it will allow you to capture and manage so much more customer information. The problem you have is that it is the IT team who are building the system and gathering the requirements, and no one on the business side has the expertise. You may even have paid hundreds of thousands in consultancy fees to have someone design it for you. Think about the last system you rolled out—how often did you realise the benefits promised? Did you get the value add to your customer, or did you disrupt your organisation with non-billable training and an increase in handle times? This is a far more likely result, and the reason is that technology does not solve problems, processes do. First you must have a way of doing something, and then your technology enhances that and expands the scope.

Mistake Number 10 — Accept the average

Driving performance based on averages will not give you a true reflection of your business. This applies to the performance of your team as managers of their business, and to the performance of any individual key performance indicator. It is managing the outliers that really applies. Learning from those that perform exceptionally well, and taking immediate action on those that don't. Doing this will raise your average naturally anyway!

Chapter 2

The Role of Vision

Given how many businesses there are out there, competing in the same market and promising the same results, what is it that will distinguish between a company that can deliver on its commitments and one that will eventually fail because it can't?

It comes down to the leader of the organisation—the person determining the direction and reinforcing the decisions. Why do we need a leader? What qualities does a leader need to demonstrate to make an organisation successful? In fact, many books have been written on leadership and what makes a great leader (*Principle Centred Leadership*, by Stephen R. Covey, is an example). We have many case studies on those who have been evaluated as successful (such as Robert Slater's *Jack Welch and the GE Way*), and books that counter the standard theories (like *First Break all the Rules*, by Marcus Buckingham and Curt Coffman). Is there a common thread running through these books that promises, "You will be a great leader if..."? In reality, there is little in terms of a common thread, other than a general consensus that in order to be a great company you need a great leader. The definition of "great" comes down to interpretation.

There is, however, a common binding principle in all of these books. The fundamental building block of great leadership is a clear vision.

In order to be successful, any organisation must have a clear vision of what it wants to be. This vision is usually driven from the person at the top, and, in fact, can only be set by the person at the top. But what role does vision really play in an organisation? Does it really need one to be successful?

Vision is key—it gives the direction that every employee of the organisation needs to use in its decision making process. We are not talking about a written vision statement (these often do not match the true vision of those leading the organisation) but the core drivers of where the business is going. This vision sets the organisational culture. What happens if someone fails to hit a performance target for their division/team? The vision of the leader dictates this, and thus dictates the way individual employees strive to hit targets or deal with failure. How do you expect your managers to behave? Do you really want to know what is going on or do you want people to tell you what you want to hear? What happens when you have a performance appraisal—which areas are you most likely to be challenged/complimented on?

The interesting point of note here is that the "person at the top" does not have to be the CEO. It can be the person in charge of the operations side, the Chief Operating Officer or equivalent. It has to be the person driving the approach who has the full authority to make decisions, control the budget, hire and fire. If, for example, you have an internal helpdesk it will be possible for the head of the internal helpdesk to lead this provided they have been given sufficient authority.

We once had a vision statement that read, "Think like a customer." On the surface this is nice—simple, to the point, focused on the customer and easy to communicate to every level of the organisation. The problem comes when you look at how we interpret this. Are we being told to get frustrated and complain a lot? To have limited patience? To expect benefits in return for loyalty? At the same time it was communicating this simple phrase, all management communication was around growth of the organisation, making money and minimising attrition in the workforce. Management and employee behaviour can not be aligned unless driven from the top. Although we had a clear vision written down on paper, in reality our vision was driven by the need to make money by reducing costs. The customer really did not have a place in this strategy.

So we need a vision and, indeed, a person with a vision, and we need it to make sense, be easy to communicate and be consistently reinforced by actions. Not too difficult, really! Each action we take, each improvement made—in fact, everything that goes on in the organisation—will be evaluated against that vision. What is most important - making money or satisfying customers? Your written Mission Statement will usually not be as bold as to state "Make Lots of Money" as the core ideal. It is more likely to read something along the lines of "World Class Customer Service." So when you review your performance as a management team, think about what gets the biggest reaction— missing your financial goals or failing on customer satisfaction? I think I can guess the answer!

Setting and communicating direction

Now, what is the best approach to take in setting direction for an organisation? I am not going to outline the best vision or set of values that an organisation should use. These will differ greatly depending on how your business is driven. However, if you want to have any guarantee of success in your organisation you must set out a vision that your organisation can follow. This applies whether you have one site or many.

The difficulty here is that it can be notoriously difficult to get these "visionaries" to put their ideas down on paper. The person at the top expressing their views is not enough—you need to cover how this ideal translates throughout the organisation, including how new hires get a feel for the organisation they have joined and what they are supposed to do.

Here is a clue as to how you should structure the communication of this vision:

1. Vision & values of person at the top

2. Corporate Vision/Mission

What
A brief summary of how point 1 turns into direction for the whole organisation.

Should address
1. How you will know you are doing it right
2. How you compare to the market
3. What is the cost/price band you want to be in
4. What level of service do you want to deliver to your customer

EXAMPLE
Good: Be the best in the contact centre market at delivering the highest quality, most consistent customer service at the lowest cost.

Bad: Treat customers like they are Number 1.

3. Corporate Business Plan

What
A detailed plan covering all key areas of focus including which department will own the actions and an overall measure of where you are aiming for

Should address
1. How?
2. Who?
3. When? (High Level)
4. How will you know you have hit it?

EXAMPLE
Good:
1. Achieve EBITDA of 20% by the end of the year
2. Achieve over 80% on all customer satisfaction surveys by Q1 next year

Bad: Achieve high levels of Client Satisfaction by the end of the year

Does it work?

Employee Satisfaction Survey
Customer Satisfaction Survey
Client Satisfaction Survey

Figure 1: How the vision flows

Now using this moving forward:

1. You may identify in your review of the plan that as a result of achieving your goal of reducing annual attrition by 20% you have also achieved your budgeted margin. This means that as you budget for next year, it will be easier to set attrition goals, and to see the impact of reducing attrition even further.

2. You may notice that your customer satisfaction trend is in the wrong direction i.e.,getting worse. This is driving an increase in repeat calls. As you are paid on a per-call basis, your revenue may have come in a little higher than budget this year. If you improve your quality next year, this will reduce your revenue. It is easy to misunderstand this principle. If it is not reviewed in this way, you may find a lot of confusion in an organisation that is apparently becoming successful and yet the revenue is on the decline.

These are examples of how measuring performance against your vision and plans can have a clear input into an accurate budgeting process.

This approach creates a practical solution to delivering on an ideal. Because the corporate plan gets right into the action level of detail, you have some reassurance that the different levels of your organisation are at least attempting to act in line with the vision. It also holds the senior management accountable for communicating the vision in a structured way, as opposed to assuming that because they talk the talk, the organisation must be walking the walk. If your leader feels they have communicated a clear vision but failed to structure the communication as detailed above, the result could be a very disheartened leader who can't understand why the organisation is not responding as they would like, or you may find a load of posters but little behaviour in support of them.

The other advantage of this approach is that it can be used to simplify the process of producing an annual budget. Reviewing the Vision Statement and Business Plan throughout the year allows you to establish whether you are on track with your performance goals. It can then feed into a series of budget assumptions.

In addition, if followed, the satisfaction survey process can keep you true to the intentions you have described in the plan. You should ensure that the design of the surveys includes the mechanism to track key elements back to your Vision/Mission statement. In addition to a quarterly review of progress against the plan, this can also be used as a measurement of achievement to plan. It also helps to avoid the common mistake of only focussing on achievement to budget! In this example, both employee satisfaction and customer satisfaction are going to become critical measures of success in deploying the vision, and a lot of attention should be given to them.

Where to next?

Having determined that vision is important, and established how a vision can be deployed and communicated in an organisation, we now have to recognise that it is not sufficient in itself. Good ideas are the starting point; however, the larger your organisation becomes, the more critical it becomes to establish a framework for execution around which everyone can work. It is at this point that organisations typically adopt a quality or performance management framework such as COPC® , ISO or Six Sigma. Some organisations even feel the need to develop their own approach. The reason for this is that as the organisation gets larger, it moves beyond the abilities and the scope of influence of key individuals. A company can become very successful when there are a few key people, all talented and all passionate about an approach, who can directly influence everything that goes on. However, as a company increases in size, the ability of these individuals to influence actions and the decision making process becomes watered down—and it is at this point that an organisation will either fail, or turn to some form of structure to facilitate the sharing of the knowledge.

This is often a critical point for the leader of an organisation. It takes honesty to recognise the point at which your organisation has grown beyond the ability of your core team to control. How do you recognise that point at which your influence is no longer enough to ensure that everything goes as you would like?

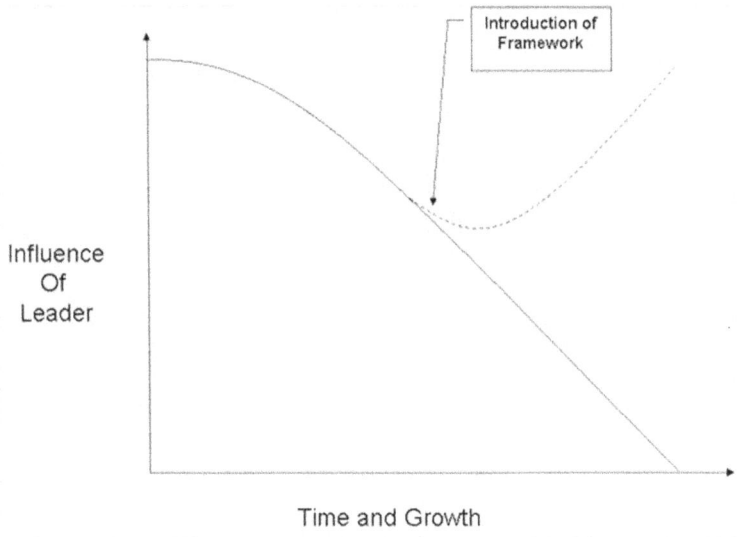

Figure 2: How to execute on the Vision

So there is a point in time, as the company grows, when the sphere of influence of any one individual declines. At this point in your organisation you need to introduce the framework. Whilst there is no clear formula for what that point is, there are some clues you can watch out for.

1)   Ever get the feeling that if you don't do something yourself or get involved directly, you can't get it done properly?

2) Ever looked at your core management team and wondered what would happen if one of them was to leave? Maybe you get a sense for this if one of them goes on holiday for 2-3 weeks. How do things work in the manager's absence? Do decisions still get made?

3) If you have multiple sites, do you find that there are one or two that you always take clients to? Does it bring you out in a cold sweat if the client asks to visit a site that is not in your list?

4) Have you just found out that some process your whole team committed to deploying has devolved into various forms that bear no relationship to the original? Maybe you agreed on an approach for conducting performance appraisals but now find that the appraisals have all been tailored to an individual manager's preference.

5) Do you feel like you are stuck in a performance loop where you can only focus on speed, quality or efficiency, and that whichever you fix leaves the others struggling?

These are all really good clues that your organisation is ready for a framework to allow you to execute on your vision. Let's look at it another way.

Imagine you want to move into real estate, and that you want to build a series of houses for resale. As you are not familiar with the market, you decide to involve a bunch of different builders in building your houses.

You have a clear idea of what you want. This is your vision: you want a 4-bedroom house, with 3 bathrooms and a good-sized kitchen and garden. You want the houses to be modern but to look a little old-fashioned. What will your first street of houses look like?

Figure 3: Your Vision in houses

Let's face it—would you really go into a project like this without producing the blueprints for your houses that includes detailed plans on what material should be used? If you did not go into that level of detail, it would not be your vision that would build the house, but rather the visions of the builders. Some of the houses might be pretty good, but some might be terrible. In the same way that you could not accept responsibility for the bad houses, neither could you take credit for the really nice ones. This is the same when you look at your vision and how it works with your framework.

Equally, you could not go ahead and plan the building of the new houses by looking at the fact that the people buying the houses want nice kitchens. This would mean that as long as you put in a nice kitchen, your houses will sell, right? Obviously, this is not the case. You must put in place a good solid foundation and build a high quality, robust basic house before you can add the trimmings such as a nice kitchen. However, how many of your customers will specify that what they want is a good foundation? This is a given in the process.

Okay—so we get the message. Got vision—going nowhere without a framework!

Chapter 3

Building a framework that is consistent with your vision

The good news now is that having established a clear approach to vision in an organisation we have the means to drive the organisation forward. However, you may have noticed in Figure 1 that the diagram ends with a "?." When looking at this approach it is clear that there is a level of detail missing, i.e., how to get this out on the floor, right down to the agent level. This is where you need a framework.

You need both elements here:

1. You need a vision that is communicated; and
2. You need a framework to execute the vision.

If either is missing it will mean the failure of the contact centre. This is not a catastrophic failure. You may look at your organisation/helpdesk and think to yourself, "That can't be true, because what I have is working perfectly well," and you may indeed be right. However you may also find:

1. You have 1 or 2 very good people. Think where you would be without them. Do you believe this would still work as well? Your success should be built on more than a couple of key people—after all, they might leave!
2. Are you really sure you are doing okay? How do you know?

3.   Do you think you can recreate the same success if you move location, expand, and change clients? i.e. is your success based on stability? If you are expecting to remain stable then I guess you need not worry, but few companies plan to remain static—most want to either grow to a greater market share or gain greater efficiency from what they already have. If this is not true, then why the big trend in offshoring? Note that this applies equally to internal helpdesks and outsourced contact centres.

That your customer service business unit is failing may not be obvious, and may not become obvious for a long time—in fact, it may not become obvious until it is too late. Too late here means you have lost 1 or more of your clients! This links back to when we looked at building a house earlier. Just because one of the houses is exactly how you wanted it, does not mean all of the others will be.

So when you look at the market, the basic concept is quite straightforward: Companies are competing for the loyalty of customers that deliver them the highest value. In order to do so brand loyalty has to be built through the delivery of both differentiating products and customer services. Traditionally the focus is on a differentiating product, but the issue arises when all the promises made in the marketplace to acquire customers need to be put into practice - when the actual delivery of the customer service has to take place. Consider the following two scenarios:

- When was the last time you made a commitment in your contact centre to meet the service level?. This is fundamental, right? All of us have at least service level in the contract—after all, this is what we do best! Answering the calls with agreed-upon speed. Now, did you hit it? Monthly? (Easy), weekly (getting harder), daily (hmm...really?) how about by interval, every hour? Can you even tell? So when you made your promises, was the expectation that every customer would get answered in a certain timeframe? Or was it okay to have bad days, or even miss every lunchtime, because that is a really tough time of day, right? Now, what if you knew that the president of your company would be contacting your desk over lunchtime this week. Would you still miss the service level over lunchtime? Why change? Or is this a more value-added customer?

- How many times have you been to McDonalds and been forced to wait in a queue? What are those parking bays for in a drive-through? This is fast food that often misses out on the fast bit. Now think, do McDonalds make any speed promises to you? Advertising focuses on the quality of the product and on the toys in the kids' packs. As customers it is our expectation that we will get "fast food," but this is not promised to us. In this situation there is an inherent expectation of a service, despite the fact that no direct promise has been made. So we not only have to deliver on direct promises, but also on the assumptions the customer already holds on the service we will provide. If we aren't able to do that, then we need to re-communicate what we can achieve very clearly!

The problem is the alignment among the customer's needs, the needs of the business and the needs of the contact centre—which acts as the "middleman" in the equation.

In fact, not only is the contact centre in the middle, it is also potentially a barrier between the business and the customer—preventing one from interacting directly with the other. This is a very powerful and potentially damaging position to be in. Because of this relationship, most contact centres, either in-house or outsourced, are regarded as overhead—a necessary evil. However, look at it a different way; the contact centre is a great tool with which to execute strategy, test the market, and consolidate customer feedback that may otherwise have nowhere to go.

And what about the role of the customer in all of this? All the customer knows is that they have a question or they want to place an order. Mostly they are phoning because a company has failed to deliver on their expectations. They do not know that they may not be talking to the actual company. They don't know that the person they are talking to is a student who only works part-time, that they only started last week and this is the first customer they have dealt with. They are also unaware of what their status is with the organisation they are phoning. Are they a valued customer, or is the company happy to lose them as a customer? What is the potential in that one contact?

Assuming that most organisations have a very clear vision and customer strategy, why is it that they don't execute on it—and why does the contact centre become a barrier, or, as already stated, "a necessary evil"?

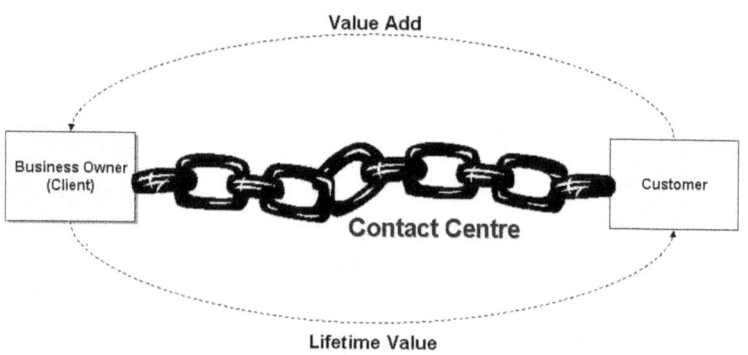

Figure 4: The Value Chain

It is all about perceptions and partnerships—the perception of what the contact centre is for, and the partnership between the contact centre and the business owner to execute on the strategy. This is where our framework fits in.

The Maturity Tree

What do we need to make sure the customer receives the service that was promised? How do we make sure the business owner has all their requirements delivered? What do we need to execute on our vision and the vision that increases the value add opportunity from our customers? The answer is a framework that all can follow that will ensure:

1. Consistent delivery of quality service at the lowest cost possible;
2. Transparency to enable senior management to manage the contact centre as a business on its own;
3. Flexibility enabling the organisation to adapt to the ever-changing demands that come from the marketplace;
4. Ability to execute on the vision throughout the organisation; and
5. Delivery against whatever the customer service strategy is for the main business.

So what should this framework look like? To begin with, it is a layered approach, each layer being dependent on the previous for its existence. In this case, I refer to this as a maturity tree, the growth of the tree reflecting the growth of the organisation. The light that feeds the tree is the sun, which represents the vision of the organisation; i.e. the framework cannot exist without the vision.

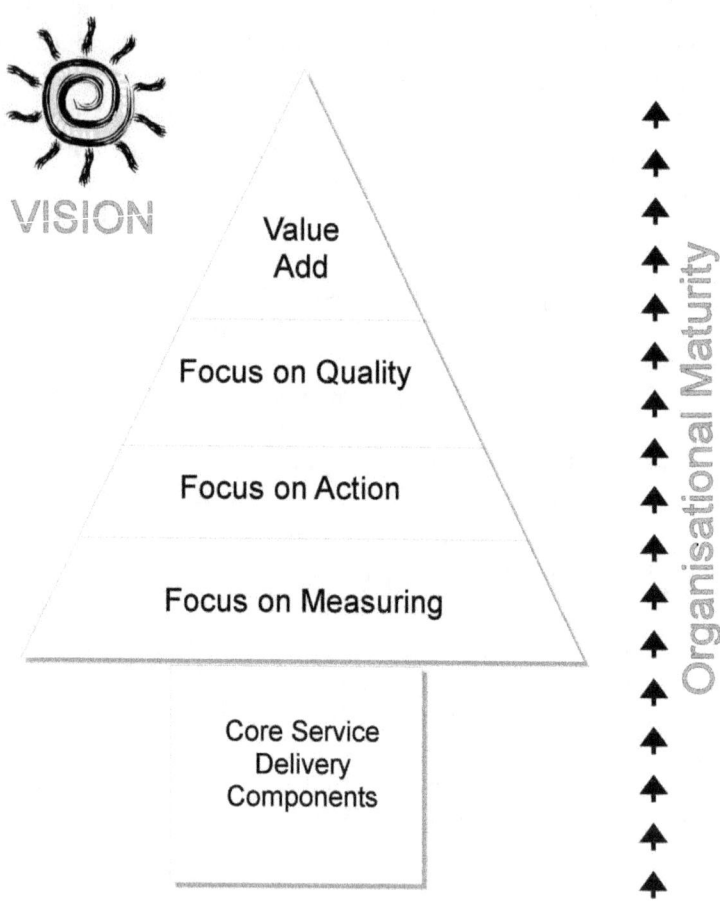

Figure 5 : The Maturity Tree

Core Service Delivery—Tree trunk.

Starting with the trunk of our tree, we have the core service delivery components. This is the foundation of all contact centre services and what I like to call the "bodies on seats." Do we have someone sitting in a seat at the right time to handle the contact as it comes in? This is the core of the framework and the piece that is traditionally done well by the contact centre.

However, this is the least value add to the business owner. What do they really gain from just have their contacts handled? All this does is ensure that their customers have a mechanism for getting in contact with them—nothing more and nothing less. In a later chapter we look at how this is not enough to drive customer satisfaction, but rather drives customer dissatisfaction if not handled well.

A good trunk with good roots, driven by an effective workforce management strategy, will act as the basis for a strong and healthy framework for driving towards value add. Without it, whatever we may achieve further up our tree is liable to failure.

So our tree model "trunk" delivers a basic, and what should be consistent, service.

Focus on Measuring - Bottom Branches—low-hanging fruit!

As the organisation matures, the next step is to establish clear measurements which enable the contact centre to understand its performance in delivering service to the customers. These measures may be driven by the business owner; however, the contact centre managers should be the experts on which measurements represent the success of the interactions with the customers. This is where we get our first chance to truly understand what motivates the customer to call or contact the centre.

The reason measurement represents low-hanging fruit is that it is common for performance to improve as a direct result of being measured—without any deliberate actions. However, note here that whilst it is important to measure, this should not be mistaken for the value add part of our tree. Measurement is expected. What value do our customers get from us knowing our service level and average handle times? This is, however, the point at which the business owner begins to get some value out of the contact centre organisation. If the right measures are put in place (see Appendix A for a grid of measures) then the owner can use this information to understand the motivation of the customers. Even if the Contact Centre takes no action, the business owner can find out what times of day the customer contacts, what is the main reason for the call (call drivers), what is the most popular product, what is the most common technical problem, how long they will wait to speak to someone, what they are unhappy about. This is all potentially good market research information. At this stage of the model, however, the analysis is driven by the business owner and not the contact centre— making the contact centre similar to a point-of-sale terminal, something that sits between the business and customer, handles contact and reports statistics, but does not think for itself.

It is certainly a more mature contact centre organisation that recognises the key performance indicators. Measurements fall directly out of the business plans and are a key tool in aligning the organisation towards a common goal. Later on in this book we will look at the sort of measures you should establish.

Focus on Action—moving up the tree, on our way to value add

Whilst it is true that measuring in itself improves performance, there is a natural point at which this stops, and decisive action is required. We take action every day, of course, but how sure are you that the improvement driven by those actions will actually work? If it does work, are you sure it is sustainable? How many times have you had a discussion with your management team about the same metric and its performance? Maybe it's service level—more commonly, it is something like absenteeism or attrition. Clearly it is not enough to have good data; someone has to know what to do with it! Analysing data and taking action on it is not something that comes naturally to most people. It is an easy mistake to make to assume that just because you know what to do with a piece of data, other members of your team will see it the same way.

When I was a in charge of training in my company, we used to make a chunk of people redundant in June every year. In May we would be told to tighten the belts and in June people were given those special letters that no one likes! Why was this? It was simply a timing issue. The business we were in was technical support for products such as software and hardware. This meant the busiest times were the holiday seasons, such as Christmas, and summer was the quietest. If this applied to sales, it also applied to contact handling. So was the organisation taking action? Absolutely. Every June we got rid of unnecessary cost, i.e. people. Every August we recruited again and re-trained a whole bunch of new people. We would also release a little bit of money for investing in future initiatives. The problem was, we all knew to watch out because if we did not prove our value add then we could expect one of those letters ourselves when June came along!

Now, a far better approach would have been to recognise this peak and trough in performance as a result of seasonality and adjust our recruitment strategy, take on part-timers, take on students, take people on fixed-term contracts, and so on. We might also have more actively pursued those clients that were either not seasonal, or had a contra pattern to that of our current clients—for example, booking holidays. These are all options which are more cost effective and help the image of the organisation.

It is because of the difficulty in taking action that we find tools such as Six Sigma moving outside of the manufacturing industry and into the service industry where contact centres sit. This is the first step towards real value add to both the business owner and the customer. This is taking ownership of the customer, analysing your performance data, and taking action to improve the service delivered. This is why you get paid!

Focus on Quality

We're getting pretty close to the top of the maturity tree here—hope you aren't afraid of heights! This is dizzy stuff: If your organisation is here, then you are pretty close to being a world class organisation (you know, that thing you have been promising in your vision!). Despite the fact that by the time we have climbed as far as this part of the maturity tree we must have established clear delivery processes, measured what we do and taken action, there has been nothing along the way to force us to look at specifically the quality related aspects of each of these areas. You could have been focussing on speed (service level), cost and efficiency (occupancy, utilisation, contacts per hour, average handle time) or maybe even the stuff to do with your people (attrition and absenteeism). It is possible to do all of this without asking the customer if you are doing what is right by them, without checking the quality of each contact, without asking the business owner if this is actually what they want.

Think about it: How much is a customer worth? What is their lifetime value? What is their potential value? This is in the hands of the contact centre to win or lose, and all it takes is one contact. We all know the statistics on how much more expensive it is to win a customer than to keep an existing one. Now, who do you trust with such a valuable commodity—your most senior management? Or the student who is looking for part-time work to get enough money for beer this weekend? Okay, we know it is not practical to have senior managers take all the calls. After all, we have to make money here, and if nothing else, they are way too expensive. So the student it is. Now, our student is going to handle anywhere between 15—50+ calls per day (dependent on call duration). Each one of those is one customer, who will translate anything that happens into their opinion of your business. When will you be ready to put that customer's entire business in the hands of your student? One day, one week, 3 months, never? If you are training the student it, is costing you money, and you are not making any, so financials say get them taking calls as soon as you can. But what does Quality say? How can you know that they are ready? How can you know that once they are dealing with live customers, they will deliver on the promises you have made?

There is a lot to this quality stuff. Later in the book we will look at this in closer detail, but this summarises why quality sits here nearly at the top of the tree. In your organisation, if the value add to the customer is the most important consideration, why is it your reports are focussed on service level and profit?

Value Add—the ultimate goal

Now that you are used to the heights involved at the top of this tree, you are ready to hang around a bit longer and contemplate the ultimate goal—value to the customer and value to the business owner. You really must have climbed every part of the tree to get to this. Without defining your core service components, you have nothing to measure. Without measures, any action taken has little chance of permanent and effective improvement. Without managing quality, you are providing merely a commodity service and are therefore at risk. Without all of these factors, you can't move to the point where you can deliver value add to your client, the business owner, and report on the value add opportunities around the customers.

So, we combine the vision and with the framework of the maturity tree and we are in a position to move away from a "bad to worse" scenario.

As an industry, everyone acknowledges that Contact Centres are relatively new. In fact, I remember the days where we had to learn to stop calling them Call Centres and start calling them Contact Centres. This is all part of the growth. Interestingly enough, there is one feature that seems to have been sustained despite the growth and evolution.

Let me give you an example. Let's say you want to set up some merchandising for your organisation. You work out what you want and go out to find a supplier who will meet the right quality and price. You then choose your company and place your order. You now know that two things will happen:

1. You will establish a timeline for delivery that will be hit; and
2. You will order a particular design on your product, with a high probability that every item will have the design on it as planned.

So, basically, you will get what you order on time, with a high degree of quality.

Now—let's come back to our contact centre industry. This remains the one of the few industries where the one thing you can't guarantee is that your contacts will be dealt with on time and at a high quality.

The focus in the contact centre industry at this stage remains on the least mature level: delivery of the core service. Even then, there is no guarantee. All of the core components described in the next few pages focus on measuring what we are doing—none of them measure how well we are doing it!

Chapter 4

Core service delivery components

This is the trunk of our tree—it is what everything else should be built on. So what are the critical processes that build the foundation of our contact centre? Where can we look for what we need to measure? Where are the "big hit" opportunities for that improvement and that value add?

Consider this first: How can you possibly improve on something if that "something" has not even been defined? If every employee of your contact centre does their job a slightly different way, then what are you going to improve? In fact, it is practically impossible to improve something that has not yet been clearly defined. Even if you manage it you are increasing your workload exponentially and are likely to introduce a high degree of complexity into your processes. This means that your starting goal has to become the definition of all your core processes. This is no small task, but before you are in a position to measure or improve, and certainly before you can provide any value add to your clients or customers, you need to ensure that you are at least doing what you say you do at the core level.

The running of the contact centre is actually relatively simple in term of the core processes that it is built on. After all, as in any business, it is a matter of inputs and outputs. Once you have established your processes for handling the inputs and outputs, the tricky bit is working out how you are going to manage them!

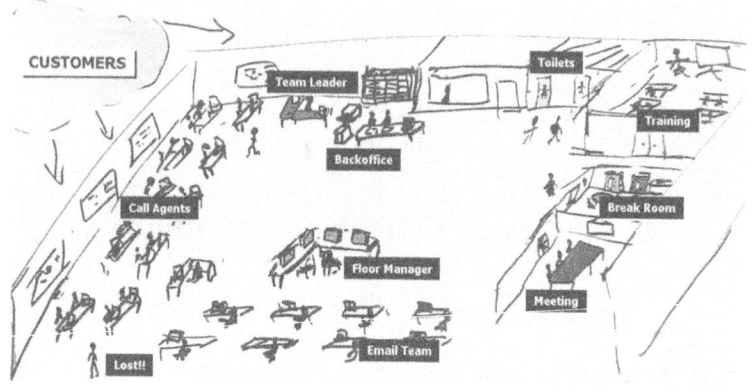

Figure 6 : The Model Contact Centre

This is the model of the contact centre with all the key processes represented. It really is this simple. It may not be a manufacturing plant with boxes moving around that we can see, but most contact centres are made up of essentially the same fundamental building blocks. Think of the customer contacts as raining down from the cloud above (strange, I know, but bear with me on this one!)

This "rain of customers" is either going to land in one of the buckets and be dealt with or it is going to be lost—abandoned. So we need to make sure we have the people there, with the buckets ready to catch this rain of customers. (See, it does make a kind of sense.) This means we need to know a few things: Are we expecting a lot of rain? Do we have enough people with buckets? Are they ready with the buckets as they should be? What do we do when the bucket is full? How do we make sure our people know what to do with the buckets or with the customer-rain when it is in the bucket? This means that the "bucket holders" are where the core service components in a contact centre sit. So these are the agents who handle your contacts. Everything else in place as per Figure 6 is either there to support or get in the way of this: It is going to either allow us to catch more "customer-rain" or let more rain miss the bucket and hit the carpet!

The key challenge, then, is to have the right number of people with the right skills in the right place, doing what they are supposed to correctly so that the customer experiences the expected service or better.

So the first step is to get these core processes documented. You want them cast in stone so you can minimise complexity and maximise consistency. If one of your customer-catching agents holds the bucket with one hand, and another holds it with two hands—what will happen when you try and measure the effectiveness of both of these approaches in catching this customer-rain with a view to improving the process? You may decide that the way to improve the process is to put the bucket on the floor and push it with your feet. How will you know if that is the best solution if you don't know what exactly it is improving on? This change would mean everyone has to change, but maybe holding the bucket with two hands was the best option all along. Am I taking the analogy too far now? You know, it is a lot easier to talk about rain and buckets—we are all familiar with these. The problem is that we all have different processes and different spheres of expertise. How do we look at this in a way that makes sense to everyone? When you get to the level of the real customer interaction, everyone is different— different services offered, different systems used. That is why it is a lot easier, in a book like this one, to look at customer-rain and buckets than to try and cover every customer interaction process in every contact centre going!

This complexity is handled in a similar way when you look at how to train someone to write a process flow. You first flow a simple, everyday task like making a cup of coffee or tea. Any of you who have actually conducted this exercise will realise how complex a process can potentially be. If it is hard to map the flow for making a cup of coffee, how on earth can we manage an order management process, a fulfilment process, a collections process or a technical support process with many complex variables?

Well, once more we have good news! The requirements for process definition, process improvement and process re-engineering are not unique to the contact centre environment. The *execution* of some of these processes is unique to the contact centre environment, but the approaches are all out there in industry—all well tried and tested, with many books and case studies on how to approach it. All you have to do is use these "other-industry" approaches in the contact centre. They will work. After all, a process is a process wherever it is—it starts somewhere, has stuff that goes on in the middle and finishes somewhere. Almost everyone has heard of ISO, and also knows that this is a standard that was grown out of the manufacturing industry. We have also heard all about Six Sigma and, to a lesser degree, Lean. These are all process-centred approaches. We will look at these a little more later, but for now, take note that when it comes to the definition of your core customer interaction services, the tools are out there and you need to just go ahead and use them. Take the picture in Figure 6 and work out how you are going to catch your customer-rain.

This is a good point for a quick side note. I have experienced a number of instances in which technology has been launched as a miracle cure for some contact centre problem. However, it is also common that this technology deployment fails in some way. Why? Because you can not deploy a technology without a process that describes how it will be used. If you try, all that will happen is the technology will fail to deliver all the "bells and whistles" it promised and you will be left with a large investment with little obvious return.

Now if the concept of catching customer-rain in buckets did not quite hit the mark for you, let me make the common inputs and outputs in your contact centre a little clearer.

INPUTS	OUTPUTS
Calls (Inbound)	Calls (Outbound)
Emails	Emails
White Mails	White Mails
Faxes	Faxes
Packages	Packages
SMS	SMS
Webchat	Webchat
Tickets / Cases	Escalations
Escalations	Callbacks

Table 2: Inputs and Outputs in a contact centre

This is the list of the most common core processes. Obviously, each one may be handled differently in each contact centre environment. However, when considering what you need to manage, you should first establish which of these core areas are covered in your environment and then apply the information we cover as we move through this book to those areas.

Okay—so beyond documenting the core process—the handling of the inputs and outputs—there are then two core threads that we must establish to allow us to measure and manage our success in executing on these core processes. These are represented in Figure 8.

1. **The workforce management processes**. These include building a forecast; scheduling the workforce to meet the forecast; and then the real time management processes to optimise the service delivery during the intervals. These processes will result in a consistent level of service during the intervals at the lowest cost. They constitute the basic building block. When executed wrongly, this becomes a dissatisfier to the customers, but it will never be a satisfier because it is a given that it will be in place. In fact, the reality is that this is not the customer's worry, nor is it a value add. However, it is complex and a common challenge to the contact centre operation.

2. **The quality processes**. These include identifying key skills of the workforce; training them on these; and verifying the absorption of the information; followed by real time monitoring/retraining processes that are put in place to deliver a quality service. Soft skills and the accuracy/comprehension of the call are key measurements. This is the basis for delivering satisfied customers.

Whilst in reality our contact centre may operate even if these two core threads are not well defined, they are key to maximising, or even achieving, efficiency and effectiveness. These core threads are the keys to reaching the top of our Maturity Tree and realising the goal of adding value.

WorkForce Management – Maximise Efficiency				
Contact Forecast	Requirements for handling contacts	Create efficient schedule for requirements	Real Time Management	Evaluate

Quality – Maximise Effectiveness				
The Customer Experience	What the contact centre must deliver	What skills the agents need to demonstrate	What is covered in the training	What the recruitment process should produce

Figure 8: Core Processes

In a later chapter we will examine the quality thread in more detail. For now, we will concentrate on the workforce management piece.

This is where we get a little technical—so if you are looking for a high-level overview, I suggest you speed read or skip through this section and have a look at the next chapter.

The Workforce Management building blocks

So let's get down to the real operational stuff. What is one of the most critical processes in running an effective contact centre? Workforce Management. Despite the fact that contact centres are relatively straightforward and well supported, we all tend to struggle with this one - but why? This comes back to our basic inputs and outputs, and it is supported by its very own mathematical model—Erlang C—on which a whole bunch of tools are built and available.

WorkForce Management – Maximise Efficiency				
Contact Forecast	Requirements for handling contacts	Create efficient schedule for requirements	Real Time Management	Evaluate

Figure 9: Top Level Workforce Management process

Here is how it works, looking purely at inbound calls to begin with. We have many calls arriving. We are not entirely sure when or how many—this is where forecasting comes in, and we'll look at that in a bit more detail in a second. However a certain number of calls will come in at the same time, and each of these calls will take a certain amount of time to handle. We need to make sure we have a person sitting on the phone waiting to take that call. We don't usually need to take every single call (when we miss a call this called an abandoned call) and we don't necessarily need to answer all of them instantly (the speed we answer calls in is called service level) but we do generally need to control how quickly we do answer them and how many we miss.

The ideal solution would be to look at the maximum number of calls that are in at any one time (either arriving or with an agent who is handling them) and staff up for exactly that many calls on a one-for-one basis. However, there are a number of problems:

1. Let's say our busy time is 10 am—then we have maximum number of people at 10, but at 11 we get half the volume of calls. In fact, through the rest of the day until 2 pm, it is quiet, and then it gets busy again, and then quiet again until 6, when we have another peak. So if we staff up to handle the peak calls, the agents are going to get really bored in between, and you still have to pay their salaries even if there are no calls coming in. This means you are paying out money but not making any! This is a good way to hit all the

requirements but not a good way to run a successful business. You can't send them home. Even if you use part-time staff they usually need to work a minimum number of hours in one shift to make it worth the cost of travelling to work.

2. People go to the toilet, get a drink of water. In normal business this is not a problem, but when they all go together or an agent leaves their desk when it gets busy, we lose more calls than expected—and guess what—the customer will try and call back and this will be less predictable—so the effect stacks up through a whole day.

3. There are some major factors such as sickness or ability of the agent. If people have not turned up at all, this means that you are below expected staffing numbers right from the start. If they take longer to handle the call than predicted then they could all be on a call when the peak hits—long handle times can be down to new agents, but also more experienced agents. This will throw out your whole staffing plan if you have not factored it in

4. Training. You need to make sure they can answer enquiries, and you need to keep them informed. This means taking them off the phones. If you gamble and choose not to do this, then the time it takes them to handle the calls will increase, meaning you need even more people on the phones.

These 4 items are just examples of complications, all of them based on a predictable and accurate forecast. Getting that forecast right becomes critical to minimise the impact of these factors, but also, good workforce management tools give you room to build all of these elements in. However, the fact remains that if you did not need to make money this would be very easy. Make sure you have loads and loads of people waiting—far more than you need—and you will get the calls. Then, the only thing you have to contend with is bored agents, and bored agents will leave their job sooner rather than later. Hmmm...maybe there is more of a problem than you think!

Contact Forecast—What comes in and what goes out...

All right—now that we have gained a basic understanding of how the contact centre environment works, let's work our way through this thread on workforce management. If it's one of 2 core threads that we need to get right, then it is pretty important stuff.

The first step is the forecasting piece. If you are lucky, your forecast will be stable and predictable. However, in the majority of cases we are not very lucky. New products are launched; products change; marketing campaigns affect outbound volumes; football championships happen; summer holidays arrive. The market may be a business customer as opposed to individual consumers; it may be an internet service with expectations of 24 hour service; it may be a campaign in which customers call only when they first buy the product and not much afterwards, so product sales become key; and all sorts of other factors come into play which mean that we have to put a little effort into getting it right. The factors I have just listed are all essentially outside of our control.

However, we do have some control overall arrival patterns and the arrival volumes depending on how well we deal with the contact handling and how we scope out the business.

First, we govern the pattern with our opening hours. A Monday to Friday campaign is likely to see a higher volume on a Monday, particularly in the morning. Shutting the lines too early on a consumer piece of business will lead to a spike in the morning. It may also mean a spike at lunch time, as people use their lunch breaks to contact the desk. These are the most obvious and direct controllable factors; however, there are other factors a little less obvious—and these are the ones that drive repeat calls. There are two key areas that drive up call volume.

1. **Availability of the service.** This is driven primarily by average handle time and staffing availability. Staffing availability also splits into 2 areas, the accuracy of the schedule you have built, and the execution of the schedule. This latter factor is driven by whether as many agents as you planned are actually there; i.e. what is the impact of absenteeism and what is the adherence to the schedule (are the people sitting in the seats doing what they should be when they should be!). We also affect this with the targets we put in place on service level and abandon rate. Do you know how long your customers are willing to wait? On an enquiry line, they are unlikely to wait very long, as the answer is probably not critical to their day-to-day life. Implementing a service level of 80% in 40 seconds on a line like this is likely to mean a lot of abandoned calls and a high repeat call rate. In a technical support environment, a customer is likely to wait longer. This is because there is something that is not working, that they need to work. Here, an 80% in 40 seconds service level will probably lead to a low abandon rate, and as the call handle times are generally longer, will make it easier to staff your desk. You can even push it to 80% in 120 seconds depending on the nature of the line. It is up to you, as the contact centre expert, to explain this to the business owner so they can work with you to make a decision on the service the customers receive. If you are worried about the impact on customer satisfaction, read the chapter on quality later in this book. The same thinking applies to the number the customer dials. Obviously, free phone, national rate and local rate lines will all have an impact on how long the customer will wait based on how much they are willing to pay to sit in a queue listening to hold music. The higher the cost per minute, the less they will be willing to queue.

2.   **Quality of the service.** How well are we actually
handling each contact? Again, average handle time is
impacted by this. If we are not managing the handle
time per agent, their ability to take the predicted
number of contacts per will be affected. If they are
not handling sufficient contacts per hour, then we
do not have enough staff on the desks to handle the
volume of inbound or outbound contacts required.
Missing customers will mean they keep dialling until
they get though (few will wait too long in a queue) and
so we will end up with a call volume that is higher than
expected. In the case of quality issues with handling
the contacts—if we fail to give the desired answer, or
capture information inaccurately in the systems—
this will drive customers to call again. This situation
is referred to as "repeat calls," and once it is live, it is
typically measured by first time fix or first contact
resolution.

So it is important to forecast as accurately as you can,
working with both the controllable and uncontrollable factors
in the forecast process. Don't forget, when you are looking at
these you should be thinking about the service your customers
are receiving. You are constantly trying to find the ideal balance
between a good level of service to your customers (i.e. they don't
have to sit in a queue and they get answers to their questions the
first time) with making money as a business (you can't afford to
have agents sitting around waiting for a call too much of the
day because this way you have outgoing costs without incoming
revenue).

Producing the forecast

Contact Forecast	Requirements for handling contacts	Create efficient schedule for requirements	Real Time Management	Evaluate

Figure 10: First step of the Workforce management process

The first step in any forecast process is to look at historical data. History is the best mechanism you have for predicting the future. Using this data you then predict forward by month, week, day and ultimately time of day. The purpose of the forecast is to ensure that you have physically employed enough people to deal with the contacts that are arriving. The forecast will then feed into the process for deciding the staffing schedule.

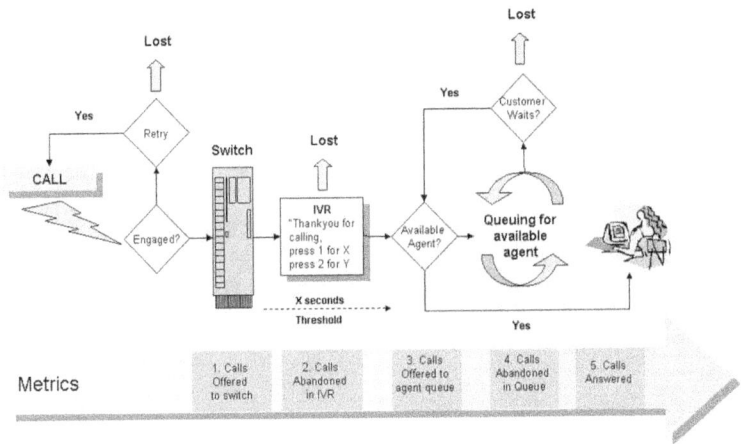

Figure 11: Switch call flow

Before you can produce the forecast, you first need to understand the basics of call flow in the contact centre. The diagram in Figure 12 gives a basic layout for this arrival pattern. When forecasting, and then when producing your staffing schedules, it is important to understand at which point each metric is measured. If you have a business owner providing you with data that is based on history, it is particularly important to understand which stage the data represents. For example, forecast data is usually just volume based, but you may be provided with service levels from an existing operation. These can be measured 2 ways:

1. Calls answered within cycle time (x seconds) / total calls answered
2. Calls answered within cycle time (x seconds)/ total calls offered

The same applies to abandon rates—you have to decide how you factor in the threshold around the IVR:

1. Calls abandoned after threshold / calls offered
2. Calls abandoned / calls offered

So—as usual, not as simple as it first seems. However, for now, let's focus on at least getting in a forecast based on volume only. The reason for accurate forecasting is to generate accurate staffing. This means:

1. Your forecast needs to be produced down to the same interval level as you need for your staffing model.
2. You need to produce and fix your forecast in such a way as to give you enough time to make a commitment to recruiting and training new staff if necessary.

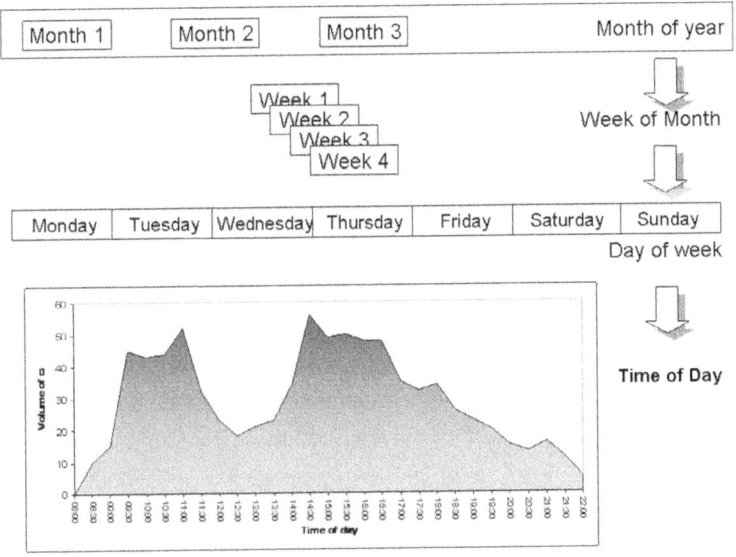

Figure 12: A forecast flow

Figure 12 shows the intervals at which you need to produce your forecast. Ideally this is something that should be provided by the business owner. However, it is possible that the only information they can provide is around purchases of products or launch dates of new products. Your goal is to find out as much as you can about activities which will make the customer pick up the phone or jot down an email. Even if all you have is marketing information, you should be able to get some idea of how many contacts per customer you are likely to get. Using history (if you have it) and a basic analysis of customer behaviour (how many times they are likely to call and when) you can generate a simple algorithm to work out how many contacts your can expect. Combining this with information on opening hours and customer type (business, consumer, working, student, retired) you can guess when they are likely to call in the day and week. Over time, as you gather data, you will get more and more accurate as you do this. You will also begin to learn what you can and can't control for arrival patterns.

Example

We once had a client who was an Internet Service Provider for ADSL. On launch of the product, it was not clear how many contacts we would get per customer. However, there was a forecast for subscribers and daily data on actual subscribers. We had an initial idea of how many times each customer would contact us and we knew that it was most likley that the majority of the contacts would happen in the first month. Due to teething problems with the service, this started out at 4 contacts per subscriber. In addition the service was not open 24 hours, it operated between 8am and 8pm, Monday to Friday, with business and consumer customers all calling into the same number. So we knew we could expect Monday and Friday spikes with a drop-off in volume after about 6pm.

Obviously, based on the success of their marketing campaigns we would see different subscriber volumes, but once we knew the customer profile we could build a spreadsheet with a propensity-to-contact that worked on the subscriber numbers and eventually accurately forecast not just the volume, but also the propensity-to-contact based on product launches, faults etc.

Of course, this was only the first step. The training time for agents on this line was at least 4 weeks.

So now we have got the forecast worked out, we are on to our second point: locking the forecast based on training times to allow us to respond to what is happening.

Locking the forecast for staffing

It is great to know what to expect, but it's still not very helpful if we do not actually use this information to ensure best coverage of the lines and best service to the customers. This means that there is a "point of no return" when it comes to forecasting. Whilst you can re-forecast every single day, this does not mean you will be able to match any changes with the correct staffing. You have to work out how long it will take you to respond to an increase in volume or a fundamental change in patterns, and then you define this time as the "point of no return." This can be referred to as locking the forecast. The following questions should help you decide when you lock your forecast:

1. How long does it take you to recruit new agents?
2. What is the maximum number of agents you can ask for at recruitment and still manage to recruit them on time as required?
3. How long does it take you to train those agents?
4. How long does it take a new agent to meet the same

KPI's as an experienced agents (for example handle time and first call resolution)?

Adding up the answers to questions 1 and 3 gives you the number of weeks you need to lock your forecast to—they define your point of no return. Question 4 should be used in your workforce management tool to determine how many agents you will need. For example, you may decide that to get the performance level of 1 experienced agent, you will actually need 1.8 new agents. This means you have to either over-recruit or accept a decline in performance for a defined amount of time.

Obviously, you then need to track the accuracy of your forecast around this locked point. The more accurate you can become over the longest locked period possible, the more able you will be to staff to the arrival patterns and meet your client and customer expectations.

Requirements for handling contacts

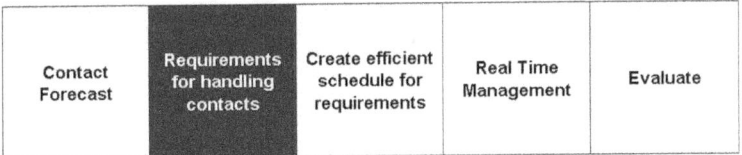

Figure 13 - Second step of Worforce management process

Right, that's the forecast done. We have the best data we can dig up to work out what is going to happen and we have worked through it to make it as accurate as possible.

Unfortunately, this is only the first step. Volume on its own is not enough to produce a staffing schedule. A number of assumptions must be put in place and managed so we can decide how many people we need and when we need them. This is the design of the basic contractual key performance indicators on the service, and there is a whole bunch of extra stuff we need to look at to move this to the point where we can build our schedule. These requirements centre on how the contacts should be handled.

- How many customer contacts will come in, and how will they be split among different channels (calls, email, white mail, fax)?
- Is there an IVR that we need to consider? (See Figure 11.)
- How many outbound customer contacts do we need to make? How will we get in contact with the customer?
- How long will it take to handle each one (and how long should it take)?
- Do we need to enter anything in the system after the call—how long is the wrap-up time?
- Can we put the customer on hold? What do you expect an agent to do when they need an answer to a question: phone a friend, ask the audience, 50/50?
- How quickly do we need to get to the calls? How long is the customer willing to wait?
- How many are we willing to abandon? (You never aim to answer all the calls.)
- Is it possible that by making calls out we can avoid getting calls in?
- Are there any contacts that need to automatically generate another contact type? E.g. emails that need a callback, calls that require sending a letter?
- How will we keep track? Will we have a system that allows a call taker to see that their customer also sent an email?
- Will we need agents to handle multiple contact types? Is this possible?

All these questions must be answered at the point where you are working with the business owner to design the service.

They go hand in hand with your forecasting to allow you to build a picture of how the service will end up looking from a customer's perspective, and how much it will end up costing you from a business perspective. Also, don't forget the qualitative aspects at this point. They will affect your operational targets (handle time) as well as your recruitment profiles and planned time for training, etc.

Once you have all of these details you are ready to design your staffing, using the "bodies on seats" approach.

Creating efficient schedules from requirements

Now, we are on to one of those areas that start off simple and gets more and more complicated as you refine it to greater levels of detail. Let's spend time, once more, looking at calls.

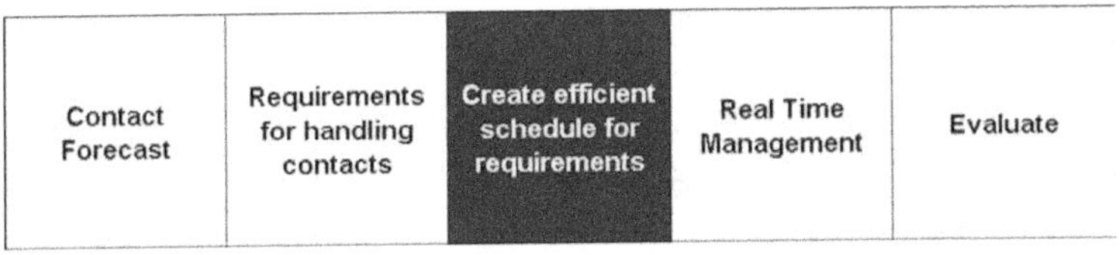

Contact Forecast	Requirements for handling contacts	Create efficient schedule for requirements	Real Time Management	Evaluate

Figure 14: Third step of Workforce management process

On the one side you have calls coming in that need someone there to handle them. On the other side you have agents who need to know what time to come to work, when they can have lunch, and when to go home. Where to start? Let's keep things simple and say we have forecasted that from Monday to Friday we have 1000 calls per day coming into the centre. Let's start off with our rain and buckets again.

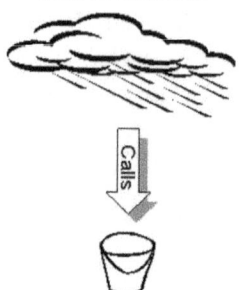

Figure 15: Raining calls from customers

We have already defined how many calls (raindrops) we expect to get. We should also already have defined how many calls we would like to answer (catch in the bucket) and how many we are willing to abandon.

- So we know that if the world was a simple place, we could decide to take 950 of the 1000 calls.
- We would also probably decide that to do this would involve working for 10 hours per day and choosing to abandon 5 calls in each hour at a rate of 1 abandoned call per 10-minute slot.
- We would also work out that 950 calls answered per day means 95 calls per hour.
- If we take an average handle time (talking time plus wrapping up time) of 5 minutes then this would mean 1 person could handle 12 calls in each hour.
- This then means that in order to handle all 95 calls per hour we would need 8 agents staffed per hour (7.9 agents is really difficult in this scenario!).

So this is how our business could look if the world were simple. Now let's really mess things up by punching some holes in the bottom of the bucket! This is reality time:

- First, we can't decide to hit a 5% abandon rate exactly. We need to aim to be somewhere in the ballpark of the target—in this case around 4%, but our rate would be impacted by call arrival patterns (or lack of!)—which leads us to the second point. We also have to be sure that the speed we have targeted to hit (service level) matches the customers' behaviour pattern. What this means is that customers will be willing to queue for different lengths of time. You should have already decided how quickly to answer. If you get this wrong, the number of abandoned calls may end up much higher or much lower than planned.

- Second, calls do not arrive at the same time in nice tidy chunks. We looked earlier at such influencing factors as opening hours, days, etc. Calls will arrive in different patterns throughout the day. If you let this get out of control and start to take too long to get to the calls, your abandonment rate will shoot up. We can't easily control which particular interval in the day we abandon these calls!

- The third point is similar to the second. You can't control arrival patterns—certainly not to that level of detail. Unfortunately, 950 calls almost never means exactly 95 calls per hour.

- On the fourth point, average handle time is what it says—an average. It is an average of all the long calls and the short ones, an average of the handle times of experienced agents and newer agents. You also may find that you never hit your average handle time if it has been incorrectly forecasted. This means that 1 person probably would not handle 12 calls per hour. You need to factor in some sort of experience ratio— something that any decent workforce management tool will allow. For example, 50% of your agents may be new. You can factor in that their handle times in the first month are 1.5 times longer than those of an experienced agent; up to 3 months their times will be 1.2 times longer; and then, eventually, they will be the same. So, where you may have needed 10 people to answer the calls, due to people leaving and a reduction in the skill set, you may find you need 15 or so.

- Lastly, even if you achieve your targeted handle time, it is unrealistic to expect an agent to spend every available minute talking on, or wrapping up, a call. You would see steam coming out of their ears in no time! They need breaks, lunch, training and breathing time between calls. If you push too hard on this one (usually called occupancy, utilisation or productivity) then you find an increase in absenteeism and attrition (people leaving). So even if you get all the other conditions right you still need to plan for this. Also, you need to plan that occasionally people will miss work due to illness. This will run at a certain percentage in your site and you need to put this in the WFM tool as a variable. If you think you need 10 people in an hour, and you normally have 2 per day off sick, then your schedule needs to plan for 12 people to ensure that even after sickness you have enough people. People go on holiday—you can plan for this to some degree, but if you have 1 person on holiday at any given point, now your 10 people looks like 13. Then if you factor in your occupancy—let's say 80% of their time is spent taking calls (based on arrival and the need to breathe), then at 80% occupancy you will only get the net work of 8-ish people. This means you will need a few more people if you have a constant arrival of calls. So even though, in an ideal world, you would only need 10 people, in the real world you actually need 15, to cover all contingencies. The technical term used to cover this is "shrinkage" and should include time you plan to take people off for training, coaching, etc.

Are you still with me? Here is where I have left you, going back to the "customer-rain" analogy

In order to catch as much of the rain as possible, we have worked out how many people we need standing with buckets in their hands. Some of them will fall over occasionally, some will never turn up, and some need to go on lunch. The new "bucket holders" may drop the bucket occasionally, spill some while emptying the buckets or just take longer to go through the process of emptying the buckets. The experienced guys will get tired arms but generally should be more efficient at catching the rain. So we need to take on a whole bunch more people to hold buckets than we initially thought.

In reality, what you should end up with is the ability to produce a chart where you have plotted your forecast by interval and can review the accuracy of that forecast over the whole day and by intervals.

So, taking the forecast and using these considerations to build a schedule, you are now ready to manage it in real time.

Real Time management

Contact Forecast	Requirements for handling contacts	Create efficient schedule for requirements	Real Time Management	Evaluate

Figure 17: Fourth step of Workforce management process

In Chapter 5 we will examine in detail the approach to score-carding in the contact centre environment. For now, we are going to focus on real time management as it applies to the workforce management thread.

After the design comes the management. If you decided that you wanted to build a car and enter it in a race, you would first design a car which would give you the most chance of winning. You would then need to actually perform on the day to realise the benefits of the design. You would also then review both the execution and design after the race to determine what to do next time. This is the same theory. You need to take your design, execute on it, and then evaluate for improvement opportunities. There are four different steps:

- Forecast Accuracy (Real Time and Evaluate Stage)
- Schedule Accuracy (Evaluate Stage)
- Absenteeism and Lateness (Real Time)
- Schedule Adherence (Real Time)

Forecast Accuracy

This can be represented as seen in Figure 12 and is something that your floor management should be reviewing on a constant basis. They should be provided with an indication of your forecast by interval. As the day progresses, they will need to make judgement calls on what to do in response to events. They need to know what is and is not expected. As a result they should be making decisions around:

- Breaks: Are the scheduled times okay?
- Offline time : Can meetings and training go ahead as planned?
- Overstaffing: Should people be sent home early if it is too quiet?
- Understaffing: Do they need to find volunteers to work a little longer?

These are floor level, real time scheduling decisions that typically get made by shift supervisors, the Contact Centre Manager or a centralised operating centre. The quality of these decisions is not just governed by the experience of the individual, but also the quality of the schedule and forecast going in. Garbage in, garbage out!

Absenteeism and Lateness

This is semi-real time. It has kind of messed you up before

you even have a chance to get going. Earlier on we talked about the concept of shrinkage when building a schedule. When a schedule is constructed, it should include a planned amount of absenteeism. When we talk about absenteeism here, we are talking about unexpected absence. This means we can take out holidays, long-term sickness and other expected events such as maternity leave. Here, all we need to focus on is what happens when we expect someone in and they don't turn up. We have already compensated for a certain amount using shrinkage. Now, on the day, 3 things might happen:

1.   You get the absenteeism levels expected. This is obviously the ideal because it should leave you nicely staffed and in control.

2.   You have less absenteeism. This means that it will technically look overstaffed for the whole day. This is also fine. You should hit your service levels, and generally the additional staff provide a margin of comfort to allow other offline activities like training. Long-term, you should reflect this back in your shrinkage, or else you are taking on unnecessary costs.

3.   You have more absenteeism. This is the biggest problem. It means you will miss service levels and more pressure is on the rest of the team. High absenteeism in one day can have a domino effect and drive higher absenteeism for the remainder of the week as the team that actually comes to work suffers from the increased workload.

The Royal Mail and British Airways have both been reported in the news for suffering with high levels of absenteeism. For British Airways it resulted in their cancelling a significant number of return flights (80+) out of Heathrow airport over 2 consecutive days—and these days were close to one of the busiest bank holiday weekends in the UK. The Royal Mail in the UK rolled out an incentive scheme for good performance on sickness levels as they have been running at levels well above industry average. In this scheme, the best performers from an absenteeism perspective got a shiny new car - this is how much absenteeism costs. You find when you look into it, that you can give away large "prizes" for good records and still end up more profitable.

In any scheduled environment, this absenteeism is a huge cost both directly (as can be seen with British Airways) but also indirectly, as it makes it difficult to hit your performance targets. If it routinely runs too high, you will end up building far too much padding into your schedule—meaning that you may end up doing a piece of business with far more staff than your competitors—and this will show up in the pricing, because it has to be paid for somehow! You will either end up charging the business owners too much, or, if you take on the cost yourself, you will take a loss. Alternatively, if you ignore it altogether, your business will go to your competitors! A good approach to absence management is critical to successful scheduling. Once more, the floor managers must be the ones to gain control of this situation. If you want to learn more about managing and motivating staff, there are a number of books out there. One of the best known is *1001 Ways to Reward Employees*, by Bob Nelson.

Schedule adherence

The final real-time focus needs to be on the way individuals and teams adhere to the schedule provided. This is a relatively new concept in the contact centre arena—possibly because it is only now everyone is coming to grips with robust schedules that are focussed on interval level success as opposed to weekly or monthly performance.

Schedule adherence is a great reflection of interval level performance, though it does not work so well for any longer timeframe. The beauty of this metric is that it is totally controllable by the floor managers and the agents themselves. Of all the scheduling metrics, this is, in some ways, the fairest.

Schedule adherence is simply defined as being where you should be, when you should be, doing what was planned. The metric is the number of the day's intervals in which this requirement was met.

There are a number of different "adherences" that can be looked at.

1. **Basic Adherence**
   - Did they come to work on time?
   - Did they go for their break and lunch on time?
   - Did they log out on time?

2. **Intermediate Adherence**
   - Did they take the right length of time for their breaks and lunch period? (The floor management should track and manage to ensure that people take the right length of break and do not take additional breaks through the day.)

3. **Advanced Adherence**
   - How long were they in state? For example, if the wrap-up time exceeds the threshold, someone may need to check that the agent is okay. This will be used for any state reported on the switch— talk times, wrap-up times, hold times, and time in aux states (phone states for doing work other than taking calls).

When setting targets, you will need to determine a margin for error.

For example if we look at a day of 22 intervals, hitting 20 out of 22 would be just over 90% adherence (and you also need to define "hitting"—is it +/-5%, +/-10%?). So you need to decide what is important for your business, measure the performance, and manage to it.

Evaluate

Contact Forecast	Requirements for handling contacts	Create efficient schedule for requirements	Real Time Management	Evaluate

Figure 19: Fifth step of Workforce management process

So how did you do? This is the time when you need to conduct a post-mortem on your approach. Did it work? How was performance? Which bit needs improving? The main focus here is on forecast and schedule accuracy. In order to do this well you need to evaluate regularly and feed the results back into the schedule when you next build it. We have already looked at forecast accuracy; the next area to review is schedule accuracy.

Schedule accuracy

This is a number that you should be reviewing at the end of a day, week and month. Your goal is to establish whether you had accurately scheduled enough people to handle the calls that were coming in. In other words, how well do you do your schedule? All sorts of other factors will come into play on the day, but you have no chance of meeting your service levels if you did not even design your schedule correctly in the first place. This should go right down to the interval level, and your focus is towards over- and under- staffing based on the forecasted calls. Once you have the metric well established, you will find you need to do some calculations around the forecast accuracy, too. Somehow, you need to establish how accurate your scheduling really is. The goal is to minimise variation—it is almost impossible to eliminate it!

The first argument you hear for missing schedule accuracy is a forecast accuracy issue. You should be able to produce an adherence chart as soon as you have built your schedule. You should then review it based on real time data. How many people did you need in the end? How accurate was your schedule?

The Post-Mortem

When conducting your post-mortem, you need to go back and look at the same factors you used to build the schedule in the first place, and check how accurate your assumptions were

- Shrinkage: Did it work out as you expected?
- Absenteeism: What is the trend for absenteeism?
- Handle times: Was the team handling the calls in the expected times? (Don't forget to take out "exceptions" from your schedule. If the systems on the floor go down you may end up with a large volume of very short calls—make sure you don't include them.)
- Meetings and training: Did people take the planned meetings? Was there a lot of additional offline time?
- Attrition: Are a lot of people leaving? Does this mean that a lot of new people who are less efficient need to be built in?
- Efficiency and adherence: How good is the floor management? Are people doing what they should, when they should?
- Call arrival: Did the calls arrive in the pattern you had predicted?
- Outside factors: Was anything happening in the world that could affect your numbers? This can range from rainy days to the client launching a new product.

This post-mortem should be conducted at least once a month. If you change your shifts more regularly, then you must conduct this process before you change the schedule.

Summary

WorkForce Management – Maximise Efficiency				
Contact Forecast	Requirements for handling contacts	Create efficient schedule for requirements	Real Time Management	Evaluate

Figure 9: Top Level Workforce Management process

We've now covered the whole process of workforce management, along with a review of the core processes in the Contact Centre operation. Building this provides a good, solid foundation for your operation. Unfortunately, despite all that we have just covered, this is only the foundation of our Maturity Tree. This is the trunk on which an effective Contact Centre business is built—we have not yet covered everything in the tree.

Chapter 5

Focus on Measurement

The most challenging aspect of the contact centre business is that your main product is something you can't see. If you have no visibility, how do you know what is going on? So almost everything we do is geared to creating visibility of our inputs and outputs. In reality, the inputs and outputs are remarkably simple in this environment.

The challenges are:
- Working out which contacts you have going on in your site(s).
- Identifying what we need to measure for each contact: How many actions in that list do you perform but not measure? This involves identifying direct metrics and derivative metrics (those contacts that only occur as a result of a direct contact).
- Working out how to measure it.

So in thinking about the processes in your centre with a view to measuring them, it helps to break them down into 3 categories of input and output. Almost all metrics will fall into one or more of the following categories:
1. Operational performance;
2. People performance; or
3. Financial performance.

Operational Input and output

Let's remind ourselves of the diagram for Chapter 4 where we listed all the main operational inputs and outputs in this environment:

INPUTS	OUTPUTS
Calls (Inbound)	Calls (Outbound)
Emails	Emails
White Mails	White Mails
Faxes	Faxes
Packages	Packages
SMS	SMS
Webchat	Webchat
Tickets / Cases	Escalations
Escalations	Callbacks

Table 2: Inputs and Outputs in a contact centre

So your first exercise is to work out which of these inputs and outputs you have. Remember, you may have one overall process that contains a number of the different contact types. For example, here is a fairly typical contact centre process:

1. Customer initiates contact with a phone call and places an order (direct contact).
2. Based on the customer's request, a form that requires signing is sent (derivative).
3. A certain time allowance is given to the customer to return the form. They fail to respond in the timeframe.

4. A call is made to the customer to give them a "nudge" (derivative).

5. The form is returned. It contains payment from the customer (direct).

6. The form is processed (derivative).

7. An activation email and package are sent to the customer (derivative).

8. The customer is not satisfied with the product for some reason and they return it within the warranty period (direct).

This is not an unusual process. What contact types did you identify here? What should be tracked in terms of speed? A common mistake made here is to only look at the speed of individual parts of the process. For example, you would almost certainly have service level for the call. You probably track the speed of processing of the items that come in via post. What about the time it took the customer to get their product from the point of placing the order? Do you have a way of tracking the customer's form back to the phone call they made while it is waiting to be processed? What happens if the agent who handled the enquiry made an error when capturing the address? Would you spot it? How many times in this process would the same piece of information need to be entered?

In Figure 20, the high level flow for our example is mapped out. You need to look for the whole process of measuring success, from the point of view of both efficiency and effectiveness.

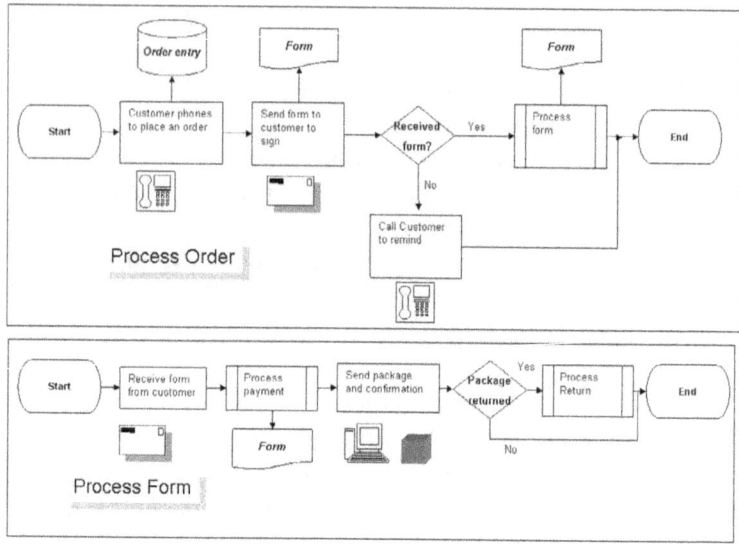

Figure 20 : Case Study, Sample process flow

This approach is useful at two stages. The first time you need to take it is when you are identifying your operational measures, both for inputs and outputs. The next time is when you are taking action (see Chapter 6) and you need to identify bottlenecks in the process and opportunities to improve.

In reality, the approach to mapping out what you need to measure is quite the exercise in itself!

I remember a situation when we were getting a lot of stick from our biggest client. Their CEO was constantly receiving letters of complaint from customers, and the common theme in all of them was that the customer had not received a call-back on time as promised. Now, breaking a promise to a customer is probably the biggest crime in the contact centre world—especially when you promise to get back to them. It drives customer dissatisfaction instantly! With this in mind we got to it and began to watch our call-backs closely, making sure we had the on time performance well tracked. We were soon in a position to report our performance against the 4-hour target that we were working to, and it was good. We were hitting about 96% on time to 4 hours. Feeling very proud of ourselves, we went back to the client, explained what we had done, and began to report on our performance in the standard weekly reports. Disaster averted!

Of course, there is a "but" in here. The problem was, the CEO was still getting complaints with a consistent theme of not getting a call-back. Back to the drawing board. I spent some time sitting with agents, listening to calls, and there was a fairly constant stream of call-backs being booked.

The agents were doing exactly what the process instructed and filling in slips of paper with the details, that were then approved by a manager and passed to the team that did all the outbound calls. The manager entered the details in a tracker and the call-back team updated it when complete. I took an example of one particular customer who complained that he had not received a call-back last time and made the agent practically swear on her life that she would call back in the specified timeframe.

All was going well. The agent entered the details properly and passed the data on to the manager, and that was that. I knew that the team had lots of work to do, so I took note of the details and returned after 4 hours to find out if the issue had been resolved. It was here that I discovered the problem. The customer had not been called back. In fact, the customer issue had been closed by the backoffice team with no contact being made with the customer. I was horrified. Donning my detective hat, I went on a mission to find out where the customer was "lost." I discovered that "this type" of callback was not tracked in the same way as others. It went to a different team, and no one actually had any ownership of it. The end result? It was never tracked, and worse, the customer was not called back. Of course, I got the customer called straight away, but if I came across that one example so quickly from randomly listening to calls, there were sure to be a lot more out there.

Long story—but there is a moral.

1. We should have been tracking call-back on time response from the second we started making call-backs—it is inexcusable to wait for customer and client complaints before you measure a process.
2. Most processes have multiple components. Speed of response is measured from start to finish; you should not measure individual elements and assume this is representative of the whole service.
3. Speed should be measured from the customer's perception, not from the contact centre perspective.
4. Track the numbers, but never look at one number on its own. To truly understand this picture we needed volume, on time, some form of outstanding list (or backlog) and customer satisfaction / dissatisfaction data to ensure that the impact was as planned. Had we looked at data this way, we may have found that we were tracking everything as planned; however the 4 hour cycle time may have been unacceptable to the customer, or the agents may have been failing to inform the customer of the time frame. The metric is just the starting point.

Later on in this book we will talk about auditing - this is a classic example of what auditing can do for you.

When you are looking at a metric report, it is like a book. When you read the back cover of a book, it provides a précis of the story. To know the full story, however, you need to read the book. Each set of metrics on a report is the précis. From there you need to observe a process, and drill down to really understand what is going on. Also, being introduced to a profile for each of the characters in a book will not give you any idea about the story. However, when you examine how they relate to, and interact with, each other, then you can really get a feel for what is going on.

People Inputs and Outputs

So that is the operational stuff. When looking at people stuff, it is a little more complex because, unlike the operational stuff, you have someone physically to see. So the core components are centred on what can be delivered for each available hour. These metrics all relate to the individual at the lowest level, but roll up to team, contract and site level. I assume that when it comes to individual performance management, you have processes in place to manage the performance of each individual—particularly when it is related to salaries. Most contact centres focus on this pretty well. The key here is to focus on the overall performance of teams and business units, looking particularly at trended data. Otherwise it will be like trying to put out a forest fire by looking at one tree at a time: You may prevent the fire eating that particular tree, but it will spread through the others, and by the time you realise this, it will probably be too late.

INPUTS	OUTPUTS
Hours scheduled to work	Actual Hours worked
Holiday Hours allowance	Hours on holiday
Flexibility (Full Time/Part Time etc)	Hours off sick
Salary	Hours late
	Efficiency (e.g. contacts per hour)
	Adherence (hours doing what they should be doing)
	Quality
	Absenteeism
	Attrition
	Satisfaction

Table 4: People related inputs and outputs in a contact centre

We have already identified that without a product, people are all we have to run our business. They are the source of some of the few opportunities to improve performance. This means that when looking at all our other inputs and outputs, we should endeavour to get everything visible, right down to the agent level. Later on, we will look at how agent level data can be used to improve performance, but for now, note that there is a difference between agent level by name, and agent level by performance. What do I mean here? Well, you should not really care that Dawn Walton has an average handle time that is 60 seconds longer than most of the other agents in the team. You should, however, make note of how many agents you have who are performing outside of the acceptable thresholds of average handle time by looking at everyone's performance together, and then focus on helping the ones who are missing the target by too great a margin.

In the metrics grid you can see the specific metrics that you should focus on for the employees.

When managing a contact centre operation, somewhere in the region of 80% of the cost of doing business relates to the salaries. In addition, your ability to deliver against the volume of transactions that come in is dependent on having the right number of people where you need them and when you need them. There are many areas of staff management that have a direct and significant impact on customer satisfaction, cost of operating, and your ability to handle transaction volume, such as:

1. If the people are leaving too soon (attrition);
2. If they are off sick too often (absenteeism);
3. If the pay does not compete with that of other local organisations;
4. If holidays are poorly managed so that everyone takes summer holidays at the same time; or
5. If you have a reputation as an employer for not paying enough or not having the best working conditions, which makes it difficult to recruit.

There is a lot of talk around attrition in Contact centres. As I said in the introduction, it has not traditionally been an environment where people stake their careers. In an external contact centre, particularly, roles are often filled by students or others who just want to work part time to make a little money. Internal centres are slightly different, in that people often move around within the organisation, making the contact centre piece another division. The net result is that attrition in external contact centres—i.e. those who work for multiple clients and concentrate solely on contact centre operations, can range from 50%-200% for the year in total. Attrition in internal centres tends to be a lot lower—at around 50% and below. You should be looking at keeping a person as an agent for 18 months to 2 years in an external centre. Anything less than that and you have a problem. The best approach to managing this is to look at when people leave and use that information to work out exactly what your problem is. For example, if it is in the first 3 months (as it often is), this can be an indication that there is a problem with the training or the support they get when they first handle the calls. If you find a lot of people leaving during training, it is usually because this is the first chance they have had to see what the job is really like—and they don't like it! Experience shows that there is a lot of value in using the recruitment rather than the training stage to introduce people to the contact centre environment. This way people usually drop out before you have started investing money in their training. Just a word of caution here—keep an eye on your training programme. If it is too good you may find your centre turning into a sort of university, where people come to get trained and move on as soon as they can—often during the training or in the first month. Use exit interviews to work out what is really going on.

Absenteeism levels do not tend to differ between internal and external centres. You expect to see the same levels, of around 3-4% monthly. Remember, absenteeism is unexpected, so it has a direct impact on your ability to hit service levels. Attrition is a little more predictable, and whilst it hits costs (retraining, etc.) it does not create the same instant hit effect on your daily service levels. After all, if someone leaves you can choose to replace them. If they go off sick, what do you do?

Financial Inputs and Outputs

I indicated earlier that in any contact centre environment, the biggest cost of operating is in the salaries paid to the staff. The risk you take in these salaries is dependent on the pricing model you use. For example, if you are paid per agent hour or per FTE by your client, then absenteeism will have a huge impact on your revenue and salaries will have a very direct impact on your margins. However, if you get the balance wrong on what you pay your people, you will get hit by attrition as people leave for better, higher paid jobs. When they do this, it is very unusual to charge a client for the training time of their replacements.

This means that you are paying out salaries with no income—definitely not a good situation to be in. So first thing to establish is the pricing model used.

Pricing approaches in the Contact Centre—where you get the money from

The way a centre manages is often very much affected by the way it is paid. The following table breaks down the common payment options for the business and identifies the relative positives and negatives of the different approaches.

Pricing	Definition	Strengths	Watch out for	Better for?
Per Contact	Paid for each contact handled	By managing efficiently you can increase the number of contacts you handle per agent per hour and therefore directly control an increase in revenue. The busier you are the better. Good if there is an even and predictable forecast so that you can make the most of every agent hour staffed.	1. Handle Times 2. Efficiency 3. Repeat contact because of quality 4. Abandon Rate vs Staffing 5. Pattern of contacts presented	Both
Per FTE or Agent hour	Paid for each staffed hour irrespective of work completed	Contact centre does not have to worry about efficiencies	1. Requires good absenteeism management 2. Client suffers as there is nothing to motivate Contact Centre to run efficiently	Contact Centre
Per Minute	Paid for each minute of activity	Get paid for work done and talk time is not as critical	1. How to factor hold and wrap time 2. Call arrival patterns being slow meaning you pay for people but generate no income	Client
Risk and Reward	Paid using one of the above models but with penalties and bonuses attached to hitting specific criteria	Protects client against contact centre performance issues. Allows Contact Centre to benefit from exceeding performance in a way that directly links to value to the client	1. Unrealistic targets	Client
Not related to contacts	Paid for a subscription or a service provision.	In this situation, the business owner may make their money from subscriptions or the setting up of a network. The price of these services will have been calculated to factor in the cost of supporting the service.	1. The best way to make money in this scenario is to handle no contacts 2. The prices will have been calculated on an assumed size. If you exceed that then you are effectively doing work for free	Client

Once you know your pricing model, your operational inputs and outputs, and your people inputs and outputs, you will be in a position to calculate your cost of doing business and your profit.

This is your P&L (profit and loss account). The positioning of a contact centre within an organisation will govern how much awareness the contact centre manager has of this information.

For example, in an outsourced environment, it would be fairly typical for everyone to be very knowledgeable and aware of their P&L, often right down to the supervisor level. This is because the contact centre is "the" business, and not part of the business. In an internal helpdesk, or an environment where the helpdesk is one of a number of managed services offered, this information may be less visible, as a different department is often responsible for winning the business, and the responsibility of the helpdesk is often given as "delivering within a budget."

However, just because this is the way it works, does not mean that this is the way it should work. By constraining the director to managing to a fixed budget, you are not giving them the responsibility or motivation to think about making the business more cost effective or cost competitive for the business owner. They are being forced into a box of being pure overhead to the organisation, a cost centre with little benefit.

The definitions of the common financial metrics are explained in Appendix B.

How do I know I am doing a good job?

Now that we know what we need to look at, it is time to focus on how we measure all these "invisible" areas. In the Appendices to this book, you can see a list of the common metrics in the contact centre along with some sample definitions. In this section, we focus more on the answer to a simple question: "How do you know you are doing a good job?" Disturbingly, the most common answer you receive at this point is "because no one told me I am not!"

Efficiency and Effectiveness

In the same way as we divide the successful running of the operation into effectiveness (quality) and efficiency (workforce management), the metrics we use to determine our performance divide down into these same categories with the addition of speed as a category.

How to balance the **Speed** of what you do (service level, on time response etc)

Against the **Quality** with which it is done (First time fix, repeat calls etc)

Whilst running the business **Efficiently** (Gross Margin, cost per contact etc)

These metrics are designed to create visibility over the invisible and are designed to balance out evenly so that one particular aspect does not dominate. In fact, it would be nearly impossible to be say you were "doing a good job" if one did dominate, as this would imply failure in one or more of the other categories.

I would bet money at this point that your operation does not have these factors balanced. This isn't because I feel that you are a "bad to worse" organisation in practice—but rather that whoever gets all of this right would be clearly dominating the marketplace in contact centre services, and there isn't a clear winner out there at the moment!

Balancing these metrics indicates an organisation has made good progress up to the top of the maturity tree. At a lower level of maturity, the measures you usually find sit in only one of our categories (speed, quality, and efficiency). In the short term this can really work, making it look like you are running a great operation. The concept of value add will be alien—all that matters is bottom line profit, or bottom line service level or even good, old-fashioned customer satisfaction.

So here you are, sitting in your office feeling happy. You probably have a relatively happy site, with agents not feeling particularly pressured. They probably work fixed shifts that they have worked for the past year or so. Customer service is most important to them, so they are taking their time to deal with every customer—meaning the customers may also be pretty happy (that is, if they get through and only contact through calls!). You may even have the business owner convinced that this is the best they can expect, and they are probably paying a premium for the contacts (which is why you make money). After all, any challenges you face in doing a good job are probably caused by them and their stupid processes, right? If you are an internal helpdesk, then you are probably okay with the senior management too—after all, you probably know far more about this side of the business than they do, and at least the people are happy. If you are an outsourcer, then as long as your staff stay for a long time, and you are not getting hit by penalties from customer contracts, you are also probably allowed to get on with just doing your job.

This is where you are at most risk, because you need to look around the corner. Around the corner is a competitor (an outsourcer, an in-house centre) who can do the same business at a far lower price, will make some great promises of value add, and will not have many expectations from the client (after all, they want the business and are not worried about stealing it from you).

If the business owner gets to the point of looking at who else could provide the same service, it is too late. Once they realise there is another option, they will feel like they have been cheated out of money and value, and you will watch your business walk out the door.

Measuring and the correct Key Performance Indicators (KPI's)

So you have to manage speed, efficiency and effectiveness together, which means that you need a robust set of KPI's that let you know how things are going. You need a dashboard view so that you can spot trends and areas for attention. Having identified all the inputs and outputs, and looked at the definitions and breakdown of these metrics both here and in the Appendix, we now have our KPI's identified for running our operation. We have the process defined and mapped out from Chapter 4, we have the measurement defined here, and now we need to look at how we map out the results. How to take effective action will be addressed in the next chapter. Here, we are looking at what we do once this data is at least being measured.

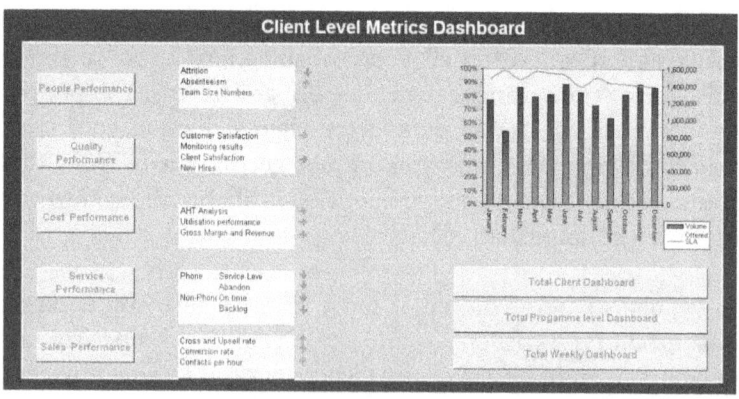

Figure 22: A Sample metrics dashboard view

In the same way that we can build a process map where we see how each part of a process interacts with all others, we can also build this metric map. In reality, whilst there really are many metrics we can look at in the contact centre, there are only a few key metrics that should act as our "dashboard"—the remaining metrics should be looked at as a result of analysing our dashboard.

Let's take this and go back to the process that we have mapped out in Figure 20. Now we know what it is we need to measure—what should we be measuring in that process?

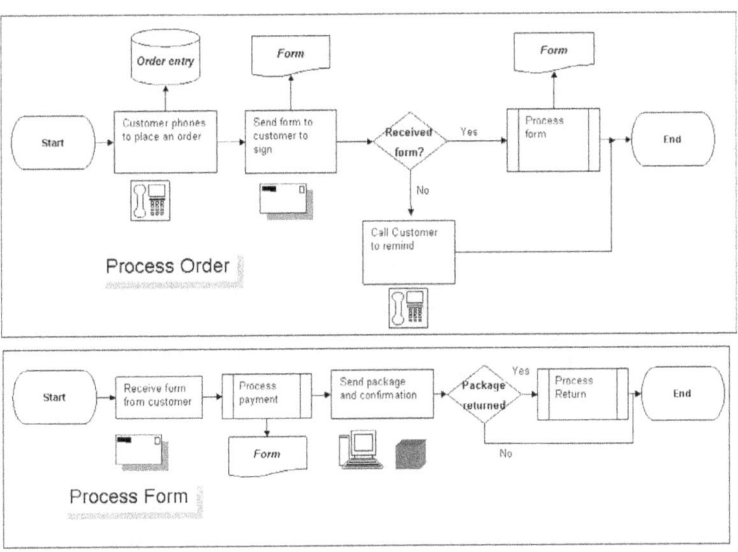

Figure 20 : Case Study, Sample process flow

Speed: We need to know how quickly we did it, against how quickly we should have done it. The question is, what do we look at when there are lots of different "bits" of the process that happen? Overall speed is critical—that is, how long did it take from placing the order to receiving the product? However, within the concept of "speed,", there are multiple layers. Let's look at them:

a)   Order on time delivery

a.   Send form to customer;

b.   Call customer;

c.   Receive and process the form; and

d.   Ship product.

b)   On time processing of returns

Each of these would have an associated KPI which should be presented in a dashboard. This will allow us to spot where there are bottlenecks in the process from a processing time perspective.

Effectiveness: Effectiveness is about the quality of what we do. With quality, we need to look at the opportunities for making an error in the process and make sure that we have some way of checking to make sure that these errors are not happening. Where are there opportunities for error in this process?

1.   Order entry—incorrect details entered:

    a.   Receive and process the form and enter incorrect details; or

    b.   Pick or ship the wrong product.

2.   Enter the wrong product code when putting the return in.

As with speed, you need to identify your approach to reviewing each of these opportunities and capturing some form of KPI to report on them.

Efficiency: Once you know how quickly you get orders processed and the error rate, you also need to be looking at how many people it takes to do it. To work out the number of people, you need to know how many bits of the process can be done per day. Each element of the process will take a different amount of time to complete. Once more, you need to be aware of how long each part should take.

1.   Average handle time for processing inbound calls:

    a.   Number of forms sent per person per day;

    b.   Average handle time for making outbound calls;

    c.   Number of forms entered per person per day;

    d.   Products picked, packed and shipped per person per day.

2.   Returns processed per person per day.

This information will feed into your workforce management approach to scheduling people, but will also go on your KPI dashboard to make sure that everyone is performing as they should be.

When measuring anything in a customer contact centre environment, we should not forget the key word: "customer." This means that we need to measure as much as we can from a customer's perspective. Our natural tendency will be to measure from a point dictated by the systems. It is important, however, to build the system to measure correctly. If you don't, you will find the voice of the customer tells you one thing, and the data tells you something very different.

Some Core Measures

When measuring speed you need to look at:

1.   How quickly you manage to process any transaction; and

2.   How long the unprocessed transactions are sitting waiting.

With calls, the speed element is pretty straightforward. Switches are geared up to report on situations where the customer is waiting and where the customer is being dealt with. This means you usually get a pretty accurate picture of what's going on. It starts to get really complex when we talk about the non-phone stuff.

Call based metrics

When looking at phone based performance, we generally focus on two key metrics. One shows us the percentage of customers that get handled within the expected time, and the other shows us how many customers give up before we get to them. So what do we normally look at? As you read this section, refer to Figure 11, above, which shows how the call flow works.

Service Level:

Expressed as: Percentage of calls answered within X seconds

Written as: x%/x seconds e.g. 80/40

Calculation: This metric should be calculated as:

$$\frac{Calls\ answered\ within\ Threshold}{Calls\ Offered}$$

However, some people calculate it out of calls answered. This is not a good way of calculating it, because you are not fully representing your customer's experience.

Setting the Target: There are no real benchmarks for this metric, as the target should be based on the slowest speed you can get away with without dissatisfying your customer base. This means that where a customer is willing to wait longer, it will be more cost effective to have a long threshold of seconds. The shorter time that you target to answer a call, the more need there is to always have an agent ready. Consider what motivation your customer has to wait and the call duration when setting a threshold. If the line handles general enquiries, then there is no real motivation for a customer to wait, you need a shorter threshold (10-15 seconds)—this also applies to a sales line.

Here there is little motivation for the customer to wait and a strong motivation for you to get to it quickly. After all, in this environment a lost call will equal lost revenue. In a technical support environment, particularly where the customer is experiencing failure to reach a particular service, and the calls are complex and therefore quite long, you can afford a far longer threshold—in some cases I have seen 480 seconds as a threshold in this environment.

I would suggest that the lowest percentage you should consider for service level is 80%. Any lower and you are targeting to have too varied a customer experience—it shows you are willing to accept too many calls not being answered in the threshold.

What it tells you: It gives you an average representation of your customer experience in getting through to the centre. It tells you what percentage of your customers have their calls answered within your agreed threshold.

What it does not tell you: It does not tell you how much variation there is in the customer experience: how many are answered really quickly compared to the average. It does not tell you anything about the percentage of customer calls that were not answered in the threshold.

Abandon Rate:
Expressed as: Percentage of calls abandoned before you were able to answer them

Written as : <x% e.g. <5%

Calculation: This metric should be calculated as:

$$\frac{\textit{Calls Abandoned in Queue}}{\textit{Calls Offered}}$$

However, some people calculate it out of calls offered after the service level threshold has been reached. This is not a good way of calculating it, because you are not fully representing your customer's experience.

Setting the Target : There are no real benchmarks for this metric, as the target will tie in closely with service level—the longer you target to get to a call, the higher the abandon rate will be. Thus, a lower service level percentage will generally also mean a higher abandon rate. However, it is possible that the service level is performing extremely poorly, and yet you still meet a low abandon rate. This would be likely in an environment where the customer had no option but to wait, e.g., in an ISP where the service was not working, on a utilities line where the utility was going to be cut off, etc.

What it tells you: It give you the total number of customers who have given up before you get to them. You can use this to see if the service level targets are appropriate. It is also worth noting that a customer who abandons is highly likely to call back. This can mean that when you have a high abandon rate you may also have an unexpectedly high volume of calls offered. This is a vicious circle because higher than expected volume can mean it takes you longer to get to calls, driving a higher abandon rate, driving more repeat calls—see what I am getting at here?

What it does not tell you: It does not tell you how long your customers waited before they abandoned. This information can be useful when setting service level targets.

Efficiency—Average Handle Time (AHT):

Expressed as: Average time in seconds as a total of talk time, hold time and after-call work or wrap-up time.

Written as: X seconds

Calculation: This metric should be calculated by the switch but should be made up of
ATT (Average Talk Time) + Hold Time + ACW (After Call Work)

Setting the target: There are no real benchmarks here. However, you do need to consider that when you originally take on a piece of business it is usually sized based on an assumed AHT. In addition, all workforce management will use a forecast AHT figure. In order to understand what is realistic, you should observe the customer contacts being handled and optimise the process to deliver it in the most efficient way possible.

What it tells you: Of all the contacts handled by all the agents, how long it takes on average to process a customer request.

What it does not tell you: It does not show variation because it is an average—so if you have some very fast agents and some very slow agents it will average out to hit your target.

Additional metrics which help you understand your customer's experience and tolerance thresholds are:

Average Time to Abandon: This metric is a distribution of the volume of customers that abandon at each time threshold—usually expressed in 5-second chunks. This is usually fascinating to look at. For example, we had a client that wanted to change the threshold on service level from 20 seconds to something longer—they suggested 30 seconds. When we analysed the data we discovered that the customers either abandoned just before 20 seconds or after about 45 seconds. This meant that it would not make much of a difference to change the threshold to 30 seconds if we wanted to reduce staffing costs. We suggested that we change to 40 seconds—this would have a big impact on staffing but not a huge impact on the customer experience.

Distribution of Average Speed of Answer: The problem with the service level is that it represents an average experience. When you look at the distribution of when calls are actually answered to hit a service level like 80/40 you tend to find a large chunk of customers that are dealt with in 5 seconds and then quite small numbers in the subsequent 5-second chunks until you reach 40 seconds, when the net peak usually happens. In this environment you can hit your targets but deliver a massively different experience to customers whose calls are answered in 5 seconds versus those whose calls are answered in 40 seconds.

Service Level by Interval: Like the other metrics, this one is all about truly representing what the customer is experiencing. Averages can hide many evils, and unfortunately, your customers do not walk away with an average of the experience—they have only the experience that applied to them. To become a truly mature organisation, you should be aiming to hit the customer experience by interval, not by average. With this metric you look at each half-hour interval in the day and determine whether you hit or missed your service level. This is a tough one to get right, and you may find that you can accept over-achieving service level off-peak where volumes are low.

Most switches will report this data—you just have to ask for it! More important, you have to use it. Don't waste your time gathering data that you are not going to use.

Non- Phone metrics

When we get onto the non-phone based work it starts getting trickier. Without the switch handling everything we find ourselves a lot more dependent on the actions of the agents and tools, such as the case tool, to allow us to get some semblance of visibility of the customer experience. As a result, this is the data that tends to get either overlooked or deliberately ignored—it is generally believed that the cost of tracking does not justify the availability of the data. Watch out, this is not very customer-centric thinking! This non-phone work is equally important as the phone stuff, so we should be looking for the same kind of information.

On Time Performance:

Expressed as: Percentage of contacts processed within the targeted threshold

Written as: x% in x hours or days e.g. 95% in 48 hours

Calculation: This metric should be calculated as:

$$\frac{\text{Contacts process in the Threshold}}{\text{Contacts Received}}$$

However, some people calculate it out of contacts processed. This is okay as long as you have some way of recording the contacts you have not yet processed and the amount of time they have being sitting there.

Setting the target: The threshold should be set based on customer expectations. Think about it—when you send an email, how quickly would you expect someone to respond? How long would it take before you sent another email, or, even worse, picked up the phone to get a direct answer? Now think about the same scenario when it comes to sending something in the post. How long would you wait before calling? I am sure the times are very different.

As with anything we talk about in the contact centre, the faster you aim to answer something the more it costs you, because you need more agents ready to answer. However, with the non-phone issues, there is an extra complication: if you are too slow to respond, the customer is likely to try another contact method, and then you have the problem of needing a system that can relate the incoming items to the other types of contact, e.g. relating an application form sent in the post, that has not yet been processed, to a phone call in which the customer tries to find out the status of their application. This can get really messy!

So what do we do? If you wait more than a day to respond to email, it is likely that you will get a different type of contact chasing you from the customer. This is particularly true during the day, when the customer will expect an immediate response. This means that at the time of writing this book, same business day, or 8 hours, is one of the more customer-friendly thresholds to set. You should not seriously consider anything longer than 24 hours unless the customer is not actively awaiting a response to the email—that is just going to drive up your contacts.

For white mail, we are more forgiving, mainly because we expect the postman to be very slow, and so we allow days for something to arrive and more days when it is sent back. This means that you can take a little longer for this type of item, and you can allow yourself up to 5 days to process it. It would still be a better customer experience to do it within 1 day, but the consequences of being slower are less direct than with email.

I did have one client that insisted on a minimum delay of 8 hours before responding to email, whilst maintaining that all email should be processed within 24 hours. Whilst at first this sounds strange, they had a sound rationale. They believed that if you responded too quickly to the customer, and the customer was still at the workstation, then you could get into a kind of chat situation—and they did not want that to happen; My take on this? If the customer wants to chat—let them. Ride with it and set up a chat facility using chat software. That way you can ask any questions you need to and answer the customers' questions straight away!

As for the percentage of time you should aim to hit this threshold, it makes sense to set it high, but not to aim for perfection! I would recommend starting at a target of at least 95% of the items to be processed within whatever threshold you set. Do not be tempted into aiming for 100%. This is not possible to achieve all the time, so don't set yourself up for failure.

What it tells you: It tells you how quickly you are getting to the majority of your workload. It measures the customer experience, but only against the times you have set yourself—not necessarily against the customer expectations.

What it does not tell you: It does not tell you how late you are in responding to the rest of the communications. It may be that 95% of what you do is processed in 24 hours, but the 5% that has not been processed may have been sitting waiting for days. It is possible to take the viewpoint that once you have missed the target time it is already too late to make your metric look good—and so the item sits there in a forgotten state.

Work in Process:

Expressed as: Weighted average delay of items yet to be processed

Written as: x hours of delay

Calculation: This metrics should be calculated as:

$$\frac{\text{Total volume of items that have not been processed}}{\text{Total volume of items that have not been processed * Time delay}}$$

Benchmarks: Whilst there are no particular benchmarks for this metric, there is a common sense approach that can be used. First, you don't want your target to be longer than 1 turn of the threshold. This means that your work in process is not out of control and can be managed within the same threshold you initially targeted. So if your target is 24 hours, then you do not want your work in process to exceed a delay of 24 hours. This would start to be out of control. The exception to this is when either of the following applies:

a)   You have a long threshold, such as 20 days. In this instance, a 20-day delay would be unacceptable.

b)   We are talking call-backs where a 5 or 10 minute delay is going to drive high customer dissatisfaction.

What it tells you: It tells you how long your "tail" is. It measures the experience of those customers who did not get their enquiries processed on time. It tells you how big your problem is, particularly if you are not hitting your on-time target. If calculated correctly, because it is weighted, it should give you an accurate impression of your customer experience.

What it does not tell you: It does not tell you how long it will take you to get through the workload You need some form of efficiency metric to understand this.

Efficiency:
Expressed as: Percentage of contacts processed within the targeted threshold

Written as: x items per hour

Calculation: This metric should be calculated as:

$$\frac{Contacts\ processed\ in\ the\ day}{Total\ hours\ worked\ in\ the\ day}$$

If you use an email tool or another automated tool for processing non-phone contacts, it is possible that you can get the actual AHT for item processing. This would always be the preferred choice.

Setting the target: The rules for setting the target on this are much the same as the rules that you would use for phone calls. Work out how many items you need to process to get through the work in the queue within the agreed threshold. The next step is to work out how many items one person can do in a day. Then, based on these numbers, you match the number of people you need to the amount of work you have. Obviously, if you put loads of people on it, then you can easily do it within the threshold, but it will cost you way too much. So you have to factor what you can afford into the equation.

What it tells you: Of all the contacts handled by all the agents, how long it takes on average to process a customer request.

What it does not tell you: It does not show variation because it is an average—so if you have some very fast agents and some very slow agents it will average out to hit your target.

Quality

We will address the quality issue in detail when we get to Chapter 7. The important thing to note here is that you should be looking at the quality of both the phone and non-phone transactions because of the impact they will have on the other metrics we have talked about. You need to examine the quality of individual transactions, for agents and for whole teams to establish whether any quality issues are unique to a particular person or are a result of something wrong in the process.

Problems with quality will have a direct impact on the repeat calls/cases/e-mails, thus driving up your volume in a way that skews your figures. It will also have an impact on your efficiency, especially where information is not as readily available, as it should be.

Summary

Dark secrets in the closet

The problem with data is that it gets treated too much like something secretive, hidden away in reports, looked at by only a few people. The problem is, the people looking at it may not be responsible for its creation, so they are not the people with the biggest influence on it. If you really want to improve, you need to involve everyone who contributes to the results. Data is created real time by activities on the floor of your centre—so tell everyone! Communicate everything. Employees love it; it makes them feel part of something, even if that is something bad! In communicating even bad news, you treat employees as adults. In my experience, creating visibility of data immediately improves it. It is a cheap and easy way to drive immediate improvement, but unfortunately not an approach that everyone is comfortable with.

Example

When I was in the early days of driving change, I produced a series of colourful laminated cards to put on the desk of every agent, which showed the KPIs of the business on a simple 3 month trend. The data included Service Level, Average Handle Time, Absenteeism, Attrition, Customer and Client Satisfaction. The information was reinforced by a copy of the Vision statement on every card. The cards took an age to produce (fortunately, the centre was not that big at the time) but the effort was well worth it, as it got everyone noticing and talking about performance.

The problem was, the centre director was one of the "keep data in the closet" people. She went mad when she realised that the attrition chart was showing an upward trend i.e. it was getting worse. "You can't put that on their desks, it looks terrible" she said. Being belligerent, I asked "Why not? The agents are the ones leaving. They see it when the desk next to them keeps on emptying - it will help them to know that we see that too." As it turned out, this was indeed the attitude the agents took to the data - and soon we were able to show a positive trend in pretty much all the metrics on the card.

The centre director eventually became a data convert, but the lesson here is not just about visibility and its effect. People are often not comfortable with data. They may not understand it, but find themselves in a position where it is no longer possible for them to ask what something means. You must invest time in educating all the management in your contact centre on what the data is telling them and how to respond to the different events on KPIs.

However, do not get so carried away in communicating and acting on metrics that you all begin to take control of everything! It helps to build a "responsibility grid" when thinking about the management of performance in an organisation. By doing this, we can all be clear on who should review data, at what frequency, and who should act and who should request actions

Getting worse?

The point is, you are the experts in the business. This means that you need to measure and manage the right things. You can't expect the business owner to define how you should run the operations—they should be responsible for defining the experience they want their customers to have. You are responsible for designing and deploying the service to meet those expectations.

This means:

1. You must identify processes you have that interact with the customers.
2. You must measure everything you do in terms of:
   a. The service as the customer sees it;
   b. The service as it relates to operational effectiveness; and
   c. The service as it relates to financial success.
3. You need to educate your contact centre management on understanding and responding to the data.
4. You must take action to improve the performance in all areas (irrespective of whether the business owner asks for it or not).

After you have accomplished all this, you will be in a position to start thinking about real value add provided by the service you perform.

Chapter 6

Taking effective action, or, "Don't those charts look pretty?"

Note that you should not be anywhere near this chapter until you have read Chapter 5. Analysing data and taking action comprise the next level of organisational maturity. After all, you can't analyse data if you don't have any in the first place! This step up the tree is found far less frequently in contact centre operations.

An important point to note at this stage is that there is a huge difference between analysing data so that you can take effective actions, and making excuses for the data.

It is a common mistake to make—you look at the data and after doing all the work you find what seems to be a perfectly good explanation for all the performance issues. Because you have now found explanations, you no longer feel like you need to take action, so nothing gets done. This is another opportunity to apply lots of effort to go nowhere. Data analysis should be used for addressing the issues and resolving them, not for finding excuses for the data.

Example

I was working with a client who was getting poor results in the customer satisfaction surveys. Every time we looked at the data, I was told categorically that the low overall satisfaction score was due to higher than expected call volumes that had resulted in poor service levels. This, on the surface, was backed up by the data.

However, I went ahead and conducted a slighity deeper analysis of the satisfaction results. Looking at individual questions and results a litte more closely, I discovered that the customers were indeed unhappy with the speed of getting through. When I correlated the results, the speed was not having the biggest impact on the customers' overall impression of the service. In general they were scoring the speed question about 20-30% lower than the overall question. However, when I looked at some of the other questions, I saw that the satisfaction with the solution and answers provided by the agent scored almost exactly the same as the overall satisfaction. A proper statistical correlation confirmed this.

So what would happen with this company? Well, one day they would get control of their service levels. Their expectation would be that they would then begin to hit their customer satisfaction target - but we know that would not be the case. The only way to hit the target would be to focus on the knowledge and skills of the agents.

This is the difference between making excuses for the data ands acting on it.

It probably will not surprise you to learn that analysing data and taking effective action are not skills that come naturally to most people. There are few people who left school thinking that maths was the greatest subject ever invented. Those who do think like this often go on to careers that are heavy in maths (accountants!). The rest of us breathe a sigh of relief that we never have to take a maths exam again!

...And then we walk into a contact centre and we are surrounded by numbers that need analysing. The most basic number in our environment, service level, represents distribution, unpredictable patterns, calculations by interval and much more. Instantly we expect that we should understand and act on this. Let's face it: If basic addition and subtraction are a problem for a whole bunch of us, what chance do we have of managing to a service level?

Okay, so take the following sample questions from an IQ test. These are a combination of maths and logic.

Which number should come next in this series: 144, 121, 100, 81, 64, ?
a. 17
b. 19
c. 36
d. 49
e. 50

Julie likes 400 but not 300; 100 but not 99; 3600 but not 3700. Which does she like?
a. 900
b. 1000
c. 1100
d. 1200

In a race from point A to point B and back, Jim averages 30 miles per hour to point B and 10 miles per hour back to point A. Julie averages 20 miles per hour in both direction. Between Jim and Julie, who finished first?
a. Jim
b. Julie
c. They tie
d. Neither
e. Impossible to tell

How do you react to these? Don't worry; breaking out in a cold sweat is okay. If you start getting all excited and want more, then you are probably the right person in your organisation to start analysing the data. If you are now in a cold sweat, the answers are in Appendix C. (If you got all excited, you can also feel smug by going to Appendix C and proving you were right!)

If you did get excited, start looking into Lean or Six Sigma—you will love it.

How to make your data useable

We have looked at the sort of numbers we should consider. Now we need to think about the best way of displaying the data so that we can make use of it.

We have established that most people do not come into this environment pre-qualified with the ability to conduct statistical analyses. This means that more of an effort has to be made to present data in a format that can be understood and that represents what is happening. Some people think graphically, others like concepts. Few people like raw data. The problem with looking at raw data is that it raises a bunch of questions and answers very few.

There are various pieces of information we need to know about data to make it meaningful. It then needs to be presented in a way that makes that information clear and makes it easy to understand how the data is behaving. After all, we don't want you spending all your time arranging and formatting the data—it is far more valuable for you to spend that same time working out what is happening and where you can focus your attention to improve.

So what do we need? Here is a checklist of what you need to establish with any data you are looking at:

1.   What are you trying to show?
     - Are you looking at performance over time? You need to show a trend.
     - Are you examining how one piece of data links to another? You need to show a correlation.
     - Do not crowd the data with too many variables. More than 2 or 3 different types of data become impossible to analyse when in one place.

2.   What is the timeframe? Is it long enough to see a trend?
     - Things happen that cause spikes. You don't want to take actions based on spikes of performance that are not usual.
     - The tighter the time (daily instead of weekly) the more spiky the data will look.

3.   What is good and what is bad?
     - You need a target. Otherwise everyone will interpret the performance in a different way.

- Is above or below the target good? Remember, sometimes it is good to be above the target (customer satisfaction, service level) and sometimes it is good to be below the target (abandon rate, average handle time). So when you have a target you also need to have some way of knowing whether above or below is the right direction.

4. Where is the data coming from?
     - Is it all the same source? Watch out for trying to correlate metrics from different sources as this often leads to problems with the data
     - How is the data created? Is it automated or human generated? If it is generated by people it is likely to be a sample (monitoring results) and you need to make sure you are looking at a big enough sample.

Data does not have to be in graphs to meet these requirements; however, the nice thing about a graph is that, if it is well put together, you can spend all your brain power analysing the performance instead of in an effort to understand what the data is trying to tell you.

The following are some rules for making your charts look pretty:
- Clearly labelled scales—make it clear what the X and Y axes show and if you are measuring volume, percentage, average, etc.
- Make sure the threshold is clear—draw a big, thick line to show the target on the graph. If the graph shows multiple data types make sure it is clear which target relates to which data.
- Do not overcrowd the data—don't be tempted to throw a load of data in the one graph. This will make it totally unreadable.

- Put an arrow or a smiley face or something to show whether you want to be above or below the threshold (saves you thinking or misinterpreting it)
- Put a clear title on it to show what the chart is supposed to represent.
- When you do the chart every month, make sure the scale is always the same. This way you can compare graphs at a glance.
- Use comment boxes and arrows to emphasise why there are spikes and dips in performance.

Right, so now you have got your data at least presentable — what next?

How to review the data

Once you have figured out the best way of displaying your data, it is time to think about who looks at it, and how often. We don't all need to be looking at the same data in the same way — in fact if we try this approach we will spend all the time stepping on each other's toes and probably achieve very little at the end of it. When thinking of these elements (who should look at what data and how often) I find it helps to think of your journey through the contact centre as a journey through a mountain range (I know, another "bear with me" moment).

Think of the Grand Canyon. Think of the difference in view you would get between hiking your way through it, flying through it in a helicopter and flying over in a passenger aeroplane.

As a hiker you are seeing a high level of detail. You can see individual rocks, plants, even animals scuttling along. If you are trying to find the easiest path through the canyon, you can see the path immediately ahead of you and correct your direction, but you can't see what is round the corner or over a particularly large rock to know if you are taking the best route through. This is like the role of a team leader in the contact centre. Most of the data they use is real time. It requires an instant response to most events. The longer term view involves a look back at the decisions made and an assessment of whether or not it is possible to optimise and take better decisions in the future. For example, in our Grand Canyon example, maybe following the river stops you taking wrong turns that cost additional time. So based on that working well you make a choice that wherever possible you will stick close to the river.

As a passenger in a helicopter, you can look farther ahead. You lack the detail of individual rocks and plants, but you can look ahead and plan a route that goes round some of the more difficult obstacles. You can direct the hikers, helping them to take the best routes—even if initially the route may look more difficult for them. This is like the role of the operations manager or Call centre manager. They should not be looking at the real time view; they should take a step back and look at days and weeks. How does performance compare to what was expected? How are changes going to affect plans for the future? For example, if attrition is particularly high, how will this affect staffing? If volumes are lower than expected, how are you going to best utilise your people? In a helicopter view, you can see blockages on the path that the hikers have no view of. You can steer the hikers around these blockages.

Finally we have the aeroplane view. With this view you can see the whole Canyon. You can barely see the path and definitely can't see blockages unless they are really big and visible from 30,000 feet up in the air! This view is useful to work out the best places to enter and exit the Canyon. It will let us know the progress our teams are making in getting through and what will happen when they reach the end. This is the strategic view in a centre - led by the centre director. This is the steering view, and it should not be concerned with how the day-to-day operations are going. The bigger concerns here are client satisfaction, growth and new business acquisition. The hikers will make it through with the help of the helicopter, but they need to know where to hike to next, how long it should take them to get through, etc.

Remember, if you try and mix the roles, there will be disaster. If the aeroplane or helicopter flies too low, it will crash! Each needs to stick to the level it is designed for to have the most effect.

How to Improve...

Do you remember the game you used to play when you were young? The one where you had one person turning and facing a wall and everyone else lined up a little way back. The game was to reach the person at the front without them spotting you getting there. So you would creep forward and they would randomly turn round. If they saw you move when they turned round you had to move back to the starting point. To win you reached them without them seeing you move!

What has this got to do with improvement? Well, this is just like the approach to problem solving in most organisations. When someone is looking—it is controlled, but the minute you stop looking everything reverts to how it was. This is fire fighting, not fire prevention. It's like putting out the chip pan fire using a damp tea towel but not switching off the gas!

It is very easy to get into the role of fire fighting in a company. You are trying to operate on a day-to-day basis, and when something goes wrong it takes a huge amount of resources to fix it. The problem is, while you are fixing problem, other fires start. You might do better to consider using your most talented resource to prevent fires even starting in the first place.

This means that you must have an approach in your company that you all use to identify potential problems and improve on performance. This can't be left up to the individual because some people are great at this and some are terrible. If you want to drive consistent performance improvements for your organisation, then you need to define the approach and train everyone on its use. This should then be rolled into your corporate reporting methodology. This means that right up to the highest level, when the data shows that something needs improving, a structured process improvement is kicked off using your approved methodology.

The good news is that this is not industry-specific. There are many examples of such approaches, including:
- Plan, Do, Check, Act; and
- DMAIC—Define Measure Analyse Improve Control.

Whichever approach you use, you should ensure that it includes the following steps:
- **TRIGGER**: How will you spot there is a need for improvement? It is worth making the effort to define trigger points. That way you can ensure that you take a structured approach whenever it is necessary
- **INVESTIGATE**: This is the "digging around in the data" piece. Understanding what is currently going on, finding data in support of theories you have and identifying data that you need to begin measuring. Include some rules here on how much evidence is needed—what format it should be in, how the data is gathered, and who should be involved.
- **DEFINE**: Get the problem stated in terms of current state and desired state. Why do you need to kick off an improvement process? What must be achieved for you to know it has worked? When do you need to have completed it? This should be presented to the same audience that created it in the trigger stage.
- **PLAN**: Having got everything together, you need to work out what actions to take. This is a simple action plan approach with clear steps, owners and deadlines. There must be a mechanism for reviewing the plan at some appropriate frequency—weekly, monthly, quarterly, etc.

- **ACT**: This should go without saying—but if you don't say it, you will see that some people love to plan and not to do! So, this is the bit where you take action and make changes with a view to getting you to your desired result.
- **FINISH**: Wrap up on your results, using the same type of review as at the trigger stage, when the initial problem was identified.

Statistical Process control—scary but worth it!

There are many "windows" you can give yourself to see how a process is working. Later in this book we will look at the role that auditing plays in the approach. We have already looked at how data tells a story, which, if presented correctly, can be used to take actions.

Another way to work on this is to look at a process statistically. For those non-mathematical types, the word "statistic" in this book may have been a trigger for skipping the section and moving on—but bear with me here, this can be really interesting stuff. I am definitely no statistician. However, there are a couple of concepts that really work for me.

Minimising variation

Variation is doing the same thing in lots of different ways. Therefore, it goes without saying that this is a bad thing. High variation means a lack of consistent customer experience and therefore a lack of control.

One of the key areas to focus on for evidence of variation is agent level performance. Everybody does stuff differently. This will always be a fact. It is the size of the difference that is really critical for driving improvement.

So when you are looking at improving a process, the first step is to reduce the difference, the variation among all the individuals. There is no point in fixing the process if everyone's approach is different. First we need to minimise the variation among individuals, and then we need to work on making the process more efficient (see information on "Lean" later to see how you might do this). To minimise variation, first you must see the variation. This means you need to chart the information in a graph by individual so you can easily see the difference. You can then easily pick off the people that are outside of the thresholds (upper and lower control limits in Six Sigma terminology). This is particularly useful on a metric like Average Handle Time. By charting the performance of individuals in a bar chart it will become very obvious who stands out as having handle times that are too long. You can then easily make dramatic improvements in performance by reducing the Handle Time of the worst performers. You can also share the skills of the "fast" agents with the "slow" agents to drive an improvement.

Frequency Distribution

Frequency distribution is a different way of looking at variation. You plot how often something happens on a curve. A tall and thin curve means that the same thing happens quite often. A low and flat curve or a curve with lots of spikes means that each data point happens at a different frequency, so that we have no consistency. See Figure 24 for an example. Unlike a bar chart on variation, a frequency distribution chart does not focus as much on individual-based variation, but rather on the variation in a certain metric, so it can be a great way of measuring actual process variation as opposed to individual variation. The nice thing about a frequency distribution chart is that you can improve the process and see the whole curve shift across to reflect the improvement.

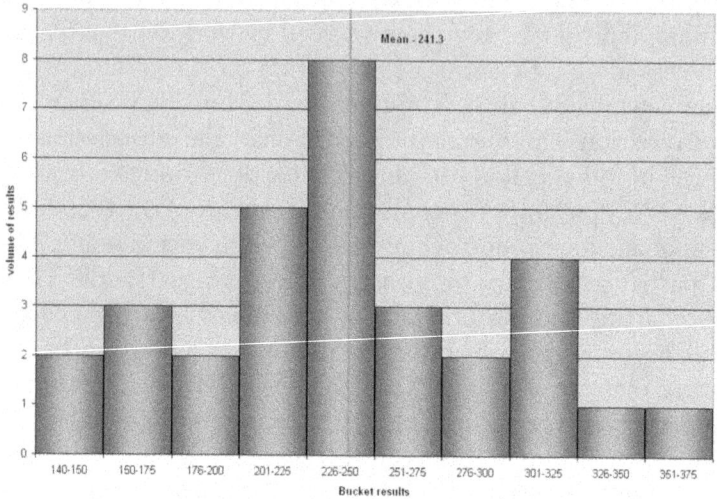

Figure 24: A sample Histogram

Correlating data points

The last statistical thing I want to talk about is correlation. Correlation in this environment is where you look at the impact one metric or data point has on another and determine that one will behave in a certain way in relation to the other. So, for example, you can correlate the following with customer satisfaction:

- Handle times
- Contact Quality monitoring
- Service Level

Or the following with staff satisfaction:

- Productivity
- Absenteeism
- Attrition

Correlating allows you to work on the metric that has the most impact and thus allows you to drive rapid and effective improvement.

There are add-ins you can get for Excel that, given the right input data, will do these graphs automatically for you. Again, it is about presenting the data in the right way to draw a reasonable conclusion and take effective action.

A Basic Action plan approach

Once your data is presented in a way that allows you to take action—then you need to have a way of taking action! We have discussed the approach to making sure the right people are looking at data in the right way—but what happens when they find something that needs acting on?

The most common area of downfall here is to start and not finish. Whatever approach you take, you need to ensure that it has an end and that you reach the end. I have seen so many "good starts" and very few "good finishes." Developing plans is also not a skill that sits naturally with most people. When writing an action, you need to be in a position to determine when it has been completed. Look at the following three "actions" from an action plan:

1. Monitor service level daily;
    or
2. Evaluate service level at end of each day to ensure within +/-2% of target;
    or
3. Supervisor to note service level at end of each day against target of +/-2% and review in monthly performance meeting in March against a target of hitting 75% of the intervals in the day.

What are we trying to achieve here? You might look at action 1 and determine that it is perfectly achievable. However, if you ask, "How will I know that this is done?" the answer is not clear. Action 2 is more specific, but we still don't know what "evaluate" means, we don't know who should do it and we don't know for how long or when we will end it. Action 3 can be evaluated for success.

A good way to approach this is called a RAG report (Red, Amber, Green) because of the traffic light approach to clearly identifying the status of each action. The beauty of this approach is that anyone can clearly see at a glance what actions to be concerned about - those in red are behind deadline and need focus!

I actually know someone who was so used to using this approach that she did an action plan for her wedding! The advantage of this approach using a tool like Excel is that you can filter actions for owners or due dates. You can also have due dates that are imminent highlighted in a different colour automatically. This makes keeping on top of actions as easy as it is possible to be. It minimises the time you spend managing the plan, allowing you to focus on the important area—doing the actions!

Watch out, though. I know I have already said it, but the biggest problem with taking actions is not the analysis of the data, and it is not the building of the actions—it is always the follow-through on the actions. You must be able to answer the question, "How will I know I have been successful in this action?"

This means you need to cover three key elements for every single thing you plan to do:
1.   Who will be accountable for making it happen?
2.   When will you review it and when will you then reach your goal (exactly when, not "sometime this year")?
3.   What is the measure of your performance? Be careful here not to choose a goal that is too high.

With all of this done, the data gathered, analysed and put into action, you have really reached the next level of organisational maturity. You are now very close to working for an organisation which can make anything work, can fix any problem effectively and is set up for long-term success.

Chapter 7

When do we get to the bit about quality?

Quality is a dangerous word to get into the habit of using. When mentioned to most people—they regard it as call quality. In reality, quality can be simply defined as "doing it right." A little too simple? Well, obviously there are many different ways of establishing if something is being done correctly.

However, the first thing to establish is that quality should be broader than the classic definition that I like to call "the fluffy stuff." This is the stuff that makes someone feel warm and fuzzy—traditionally referred to as Soft Skills.

In looking at a maturity model, the fluffy stuff really belongs in the Value Add stage. It is something that at the lower levels in the cycle you can compromise with—you do not have to aim for the very highest "soft skills" experience as long as you are at least "doing it right."

So what is quality in the contact centre? If it is defined as "doing it right," then we need to understand two things:

1.   What is "it"; and
2.   How do we know what "right" is?

What is "it"?

One of the most common mistakes made is to regard "it" too narrowly i.e. "it" is handling calls. That's it, nothing else. If we are really lucky and forward thinking, then it is possible the "it" is handling contacts, and so we include email and other contact types—although this is certainly less common.

The other common mistake is to only look at "it" once we have won the business, built the computers and tools, staffed the desk and started taking calls. This means it is too late for us to fully control the delivery of "doing it right" because we have already committed ourselves to a whole bunch of stuff that we can't really go back on. In fact, the last thing we do is look at the customer experience part of "doing it right." This is the first thing we should do!

Increasingly, business owners looking to put business into contact centres start by asking the question, "How are you going to guarantee that you can give the customer an experience as we have defined it?"

1. The starting point has to be the definition of the experience we want our customers to have.
2. From there we can work our way back, through a filtering process, to what we do to measure the degree to which this is being delivered.
3. The next step is to identify what qualities an agent must have to be able to demonstrate the right behaviour and hit the targets.
4. Then work out, of those skills, which ones will you cover during the training process.
5. In order to be successful at the training, and hence successful in delivering on the targets, it is key to use the recruitment process as an effective filter, ensuring that ultimately, it is only those with the aptitude and right qualities who are recruited into the organisation.

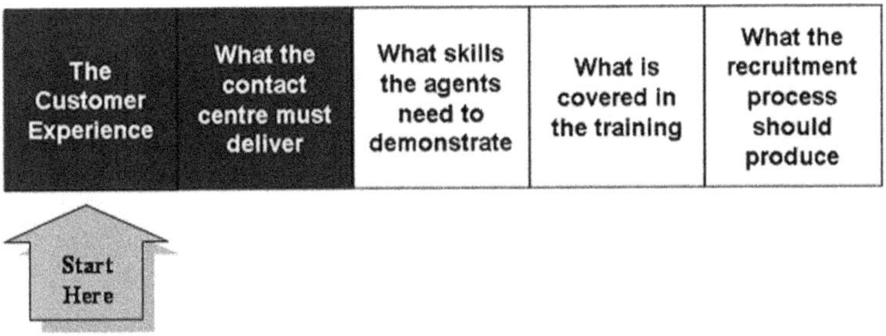

The Customer Experience	What the contact centre must deliver	What skills the agents need to demonstrate	What is covered in the training	What the recruitment process should produce

Start Here

Figure 25: Top level quality process

The drivers of customer perception — the customer experience

When driving the perception that the customer has of their experience, there are some elements that do not drive a high level of satisfaction - the neutral drivers. When absent or poor, the customer notices. When present or excellent, the customer does not. For example, the time it takes to answer the phone is a given. Provided it is not too extreme in the time it takes to get through, the customer will not even notice. The minute it takes too long, customer dissatisfaction will begin to increase. This means it can count against you, but it is highly unlikely that answering the phone particularly quickly will increase your customer satisfaction. Which means then when looking at where we should give our attention to gain the most value from the contact, we need to focus on those things that real enhance the satisfaction of the customer with their experience.

The catch in this, and the tricky bit, is that a lot of these drivers are strongly linked to the expectations that the customers begin with. The more frequent the interaction the customer has with your contact centre, the higher up the scale their expectations rise.

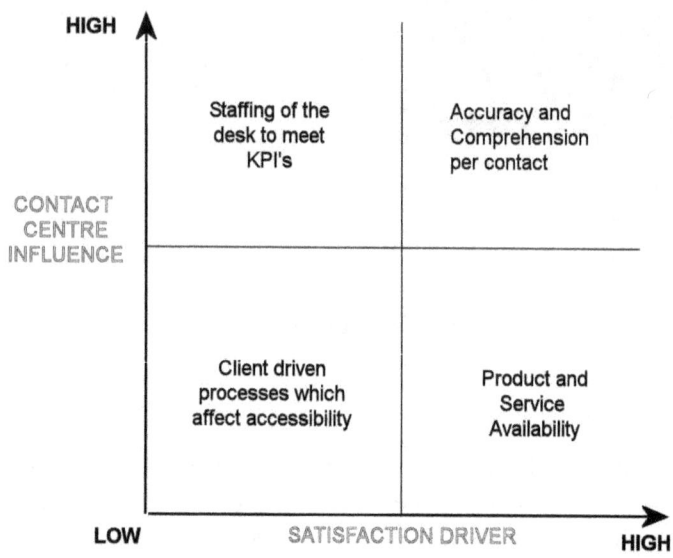

Figure 26 What can influence customer satisfaction

As with anything, although it is key to define the customer experience, this is by far the hardest step to take in the process. It requires a comprehensive understanding of what is important to customers in different markets. You need to identify the following for each contract you have:

1. Which factors can be classed as having no positive influence, e.g., "Average Speed of Answer." These are areas that we do not need to feed into recruitment, but rather cover through the design of our service from a workforce management and basic service delivery approach.

2. Which factors may drive dissatisfaction but are totally outside of the control of an individual agent, e.g., the returns policy of a client. Here, whilst product and policy training must be provided, this is not the

responsibility of the agent but rather the responsibility of the contact centre to establish accurate and representative measures that can be used as a control framework to provide visibility. These measures would typically include Customer and Client Dissatisfaction, Switch reports focussing on presented volumes, and other reports that allow visibility of what comes into the teams to be handled and what goes out. These factors may drive dissatisfaction when incorrect, but if they are done correctly they are unlikely to specifically drive satisfaction

3. Which factors will deliberately drive satisfaction, e.g., getting the right answer when you call; having a problem fixed; feeling like the product you have bought has been a good deal; and feeling like an individual customer as opposed to one amongst hundreds and thousands.

In reviewing the results of a customer satisfaction survey for one of our clients, we found clear evidence that the results of the customer satisfaction survey fall clearly into Satisfaction drivers and Dissatisfaction drivers. In addition we can see that it is a mistake to ignore the Customer Dissatisfaction results.

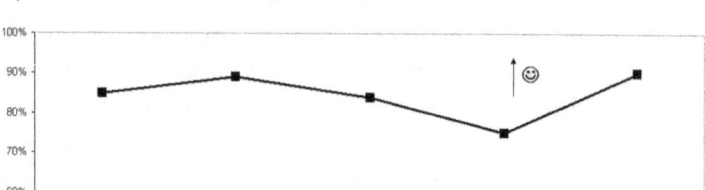

Figure 27: Customer Satisfaction and its relationship to
Dissatisfaction

The survey was conducted on a five-point scale. The
focus, as with many clients, was on managing to customer
satisfaction (as opposed to dissatisfaction). In the chart, it can
be seen that the satisfaction results as measured by the top two
boxes (extremely satisfied and very satisfied) generally track
with the dissatisfaction, measured in this case by the bottom 2
boxes (extremely and somewhat dissatisfied). But what are we
saying when we see it tracking? What the chart shows is that,
in general, it is possible for dissatisfaction to go up at the same
time as satisfaction goes up. The normal response in analysing
this would be to question the integrity of the data.

However, in order to fully understand this data you need
to dig a little deeper. For example, there were some issues in
staffing the desk. This resulted in dissatisfaction from the
customers in regards to wait time to get through to the desk.
This did not affect their overall satisfaction (service availability
is not a satisfier, but rather a dissatisfier if it is substandard).
At the same time, when looking at the questions on solution

provided and comprehension of question, the customers were scoring relatively high, which resulted in overall satisfaction also increasing, because accuracy, doing it right, is a satisfier. On the other hand, in May new recruits were manning the desk, resulting in a dramatic reduction in overall satisfaction, without the equivalent increase in dissatisfaction.

So in designing our service, the main focus should be on allowing us to hit the upper right quadrant of the model shown in Figure 26 i.e. High satisfaction of the customer that we have the highest degree of influence over. This is where all efforts in defining the customer experience should be focussed. Now think about your own environment. How often is it the upper left quadrant where you focus your efforts?

What this means is that "it" becomes redefined as "the customer experience," and "doing it right" gets redefined as clearly outlining the customer experience we are aiming for and then establishing a clear mechanism for measuring it. This is far broader than the definition we started off with at the start of this section, in terms of handling calls, and it puts the focus heavily on the Value Add part of any of the processes we are deploying.

What the contact centre must deliver—knowing what "right" is

Now that we know what "it" is, where do we start when it comes to knowing what is right? First you have to decide whether you are with us so far in believing that quality is "doing it right." Once you agree with this, it becomes clear that in order to manage quality and manage the "right" bit, you need to work out which bits of activity in the centre are related to quality. In fact, you need to realise different classifications of metrics we discussed in the metrics chapter (Operational, Financial, Quality) are not all distinct and separate, but rather are all related. So in order to tell the story of your centre's performance, you must use and understand all elements. In the diagram in Figure 28, the relationships between the overall customer and the more traditional metrics are made clear.

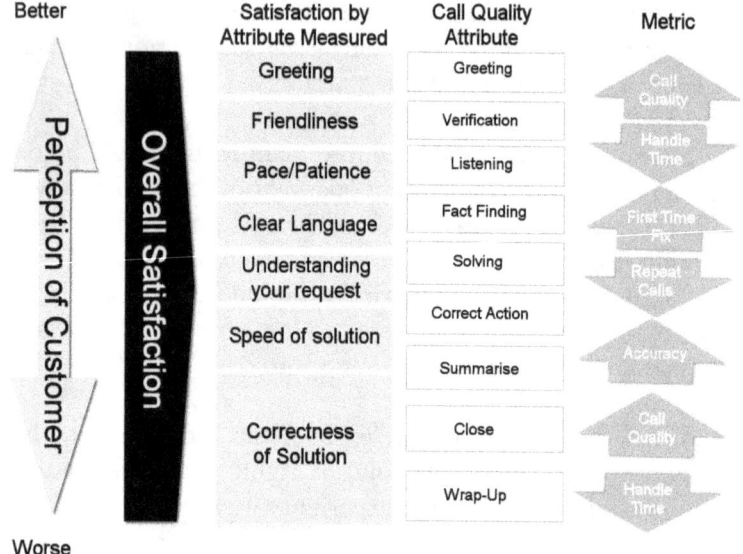

Figure 28: Knowing what is right

There is no single metric that you can view in a contact centre that will tell you everything you need to know. Instead, the metrics you report on should form something more along the lines of an alert. They act as flags to tell you whether you need to look further or not.

Let me give you an example here:

Let us say that we fail to hit our **customer satisfaction** target one particular month. This is the flag. It does not help us understand why; all it does is tell us we have a problem that we need to understand so we can fix it.

The next step is to dig into the specific **attributes** that we have asked the customer about. Let's say that in looking at these we discover that the soft skills are okay– we are being very warm and fluffy with the customers—but there are some concerns around **providing the right solution**.

We now need to see what happened this month that did not happen in previous months—what changed?

Let's look at the results of our **call monitoring** (if we have them) and discover that our scores are high for both soft skills and **accuracy**. So no help in that direction. Where else can we look?

Well, we first need to **calibrate** our monitoring with our customer satisfaction results—we don't want the same problem in later months. Then we need to look at where else we may find out what has been going on. In a technical support environment we should look at **first-time fix**; in a sales environment we should look at **confirmed sales** or **cancellations**.

If our **first-time fix** has gone down, it is likely that our **call volume** has **increased** as customers are placing **repeat calls**.

This increase in call volume is likely to have had an impact on our **service level** unless our desk is overstaffed. If it is overstaffed, then we would expect an impact on the **occupancy**. When your occupancy goes up it is common to see an impact on either **absenteeism** or **attrition**. When this happens we find we may need to recruit and, as a result, we have new hires handling contacts. The **Average Handle Time** for these new hires will be higher and their knowledge is poorer, so we would expect the **accuracy** to be worse. Now we have come round in a full circle, have we not!

At the end of this analysis there is still an important question we must ask. This is: Why didn't we know all this before the customer satisfaction results even came out? With all the data we have, we should be able to predict the results of our customer satisfaction survey before we achieve them. There's a thought!

So when looking at the element of "doing it right" and understanding what "right" really means, we will usually start by looking at a bunch of metrics –but not in isolation; rather in a metric map where we can look at how they all relate to each other. The diagram in Figure 28 and the subsequent text give a good preview of what this map will look like.

Which skills the agent needs to demonstrate (not grabbing the first person off the street)

The Customer Experience	What the contact centre must deliver	What skills the agents need to demonstrate	What is covered in the training	What the recruitment process should produce

Figure 29: First step of the Quality process

Now that we have defined the customer experience, and defined how we will know how well we are doing, we are ready to build the infrastructure around its delivery. As we have already stated, in a contact centre we have not got a product. This means that our agents are the raw material we work with; they are the frontline to the customer. So building an infrastructure in this environment is all about getting the right people on board.

Let me start by asking a question. In your opinion, is teamwork a key skill when recruiting an agent?

a)   If your answer to this question is "yes," why? What result/attribute in relation to customer satisfaction or efficiency does teamwork, as a personal quality, drive?

b) If your answer is "no," why? How will knowledge be shared in the teams? Will you give bonuses purely on individual performance or will team performance count?

So what are the skills the agents need to demonstrate? Which can you teach, and which are needed at the recruitment stage?

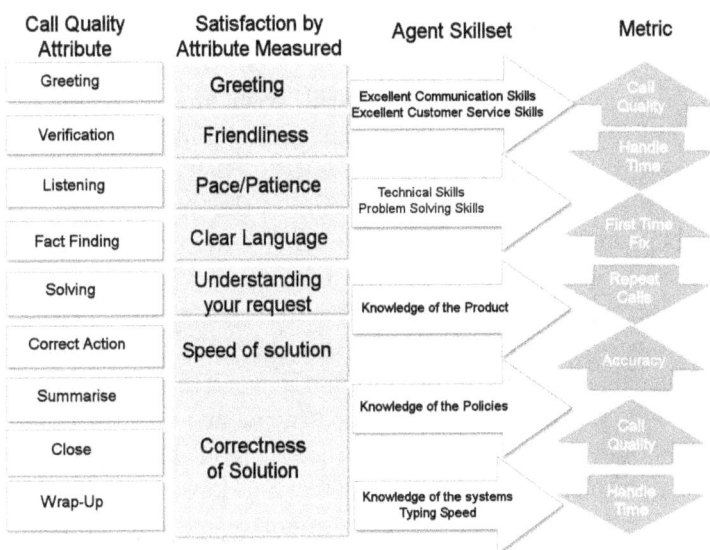

Figure 30: How skills of an agent relate to the customer satisfaction result

First you need to map out the required skill set. In a sales environment, instead of technical skills you would require a selling skill. We are looking at this in a different way to the traditional approach; in fact, it may seem a little back-to-front to you at first. However, by starting with the behaviour we need to see on the phone, we can make sure that we are recruiting correctly. If we start at the recruitment side, we can't be sure that the skills that will be demonstrated after training will match the behaviours we need to see on the phone. It's a form of reverse engineering. It's like a jigsaw puzzle: First you look at the overall picture to see where you are aiming, then the overall picture is printed onto a card which is then stamped out onto a template of individual pieces which are boxed and separated. We are starting off with the overall picture and then working out what knowledge goes into the training to make up that picture, and from that we have the separate pieces which are the required skill set to learn the knowledge. Does this make sense?

Assuming that you are still with me (I know, big assumption), we need to look at Figure 31 and work out what we need to recruit. We start off with the behaviour that must be met—this is reviewed by looking at the measures we have in place once an agent is operational. We then review the skill that will be required to achieve benchmarks in the measure. This is then mapped on to a set of training that will be provided by the operations in order to ensure the skills exist. Finally, in order to be receptive to the training, we need to look for certain aptitude, skills and behaviours at recruitment—so we map those out. Should you choose, you can then map one step further and identify the specific recruitment test and pass thresholds that will be used by your own recruitment team. This process is represented in the diagram in Figure 31.

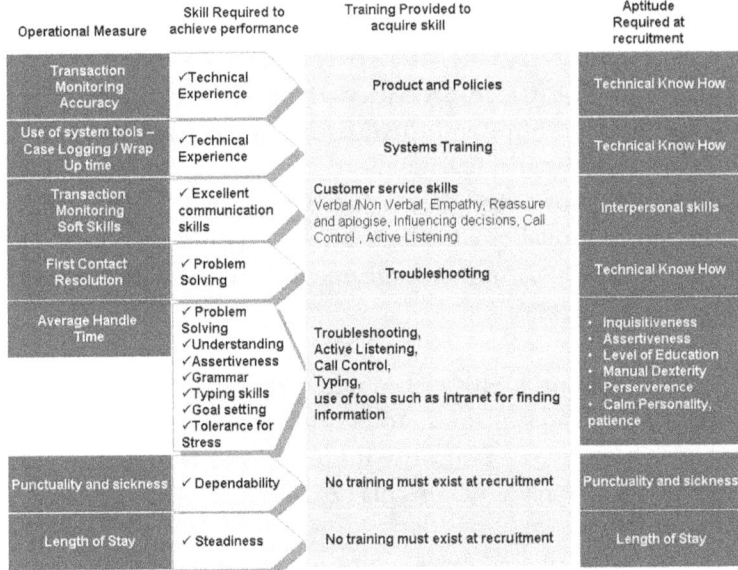

Operational Measure	Skill Required to achieve performance	Training Provided to acquire skill	Aptitude Required at recruitment
Transaction Monitoring Accuracy	✓Technical Experience	Product and Policies	Technical Know How
Use of system tools – Case Logging / Wrap Up time	✓Technical Experience	Systems Training	Technical Know How
Transaction Monitoring Soft Skills	✓ Excellent communication skills	Customer service skills Verbal /Non Verbal, Empathy, Reassure and aplogise, Influencing decisions, Call Control , Active Listening	Interpersonal skills
First Contact Resolution	✓ Problem Solving	Troubleshooting	Technical Know How
Average Handle Time	✓ Problem Solving ✓Understanding ✓Assertiveness ✓Grammar ✓Typing skills ✓Goal setting ✓Tolerance for Stress	Troubleshooting, Active Listening, Call Control, Typing, use of tools such as Intranet for finding information	• Inquisitiveness • Assertiveness • Level of Education • Manual Dexterity • Perserverence • Calm Personality, patience
Punctuality and sickness	✓ Dependability	No training must exist at recruitment	Punctuality and sickness
Length of Stay	✓ Steadiness	No training must exist at recruitment	Length of Stay

Figure 31: How you map agent performance to what you look for in recruitment

By clearly defining this process, you can ensure that your recruitment profiles cover all necessary requirements and actually recruit people with a sufficient level of skills to perform their role. This will not only lead to improved performance from operational and quality perspectives, but should also lead to lower attrition. People who are asked to do something that is beyond their skill set, or not what they expected, will leave, and usually in the first 90 days. A robust process at the recruitment and training end will reduce this "90 day attrition" phenomenon.

"This call may be recorded for training purposes"—yes, please!

How many times have you phoned an organisation and heard the pre-recorded message on the IVR stating, "this call may be recorded for training and quality purposes"? This is a very reassuring message because it means that at some point someone actually had the intent of reviewing the calls and using that information to give feedback to the agents. Now, intent does not mean execution—and the fact that something is recorded does not mean anything happens to it after that. So monitoring is the process of sitting down and observing a transaction to guarantee the quality of the customer experience, coach and develop individuals, and manage operational efficiency metrics such as handle time.

One of the problems with monitoring any sort of transaction is the time it takes to do it. You need to sit down, maybe with the agent, listen to a call, write it up, and give feedback. If you have 20 agents on your team this can be a real pain.

Or at least that is how it is commonly perceived. The reality is that monitoring the different transactions in a centre is one of the few ways to accomplish the following:

- Checking the quality of a customer interaction before it becomes a customer complaint;
- Managing handle time by learning from the best and sharing with the rest;
- Identifying knowledge gaps and training needs;
- Providing individual feedback to agents to let them know how they are getting on;
- Spotting and fixing process issues or systems issues that prevent agents from doing their jobs effectively; and
- Validating data collected and reasons for performance issues.

In fact, in looking at the role of a supervisor in a contact centre environment, it is hard to work out exactly what they should be doing to fill their day if they are not monitoring those transactions handled by their agents.

In Figure 30 we looked at the sort of attributes that should be used in monitoring, but what about the rest of the process? How should it be approached? How should actions be taken and developed?

Monitoring is your only method to have some form of guarantee over the quality of a customer contact before it is too late. This means we have to get the process right - if we don't we may as well use the time in a more valuable way, such as shopping or drinking coffee. No point putting the effort into listening or observing the customer contacts if you don't make use of what you see. So some things to think about:

- All Agents must be monitored
- You are measuring the customer experience not a personal opinion
- You need to spread out the monitoring sessions over time—to allow for different customer types and different shifts of agents
- You need to follow the same structure each time you observe a transaction
- All customer contact types should be checked; phone, email, chat, cases etc.
- You need to measure as objectively as possible
- You need to do something with the results
- You need to feedback to agents
- You want to give the most time to the people who need it and only do a small sample of those that don't. New hires and people making mistakes are those that need the most attention.

I once spent time in a company that had an approach to monitoring that appeared comprehensive on the surface. It had lots of pretty documentation and even a graphic to represent the approach to monitoring. The problem was, there was no scoring of the monitoring sessions. This meant that everyone was cursed with "perpetual feedback and coaching" every time something was not up to scratch. The lack of scoring meant that they could not follow through on the effectiveness of the coaching. It also meant they could not relate what they found to what the customer wanted. At the end of the day, the quality was not really controlled and their time would have been more effectively spent drinking coffee and chatting!

So it is important to design your monitoring form correctly to allow you measure and compare and also to make sure you are capturing the stuff that is a big deal to your customers - in Six Sigma terminology this is referred to as "Critical to Quality (CTQ)"

How should you approach designing these attributes and your scoring? Well there are a number of possible approaches, but this is not something that should be done in isolation. The business owner should be able to define the customer experience (you should have already done this for recruiting purposes!) and this is the first input into the monitoring form. Next you have to reflect the company values (remember way back in the second chapter?). The monitoring form gives you an opportunity to reinforce what is important to your company. This is particularly important if you are an outsource organisation that has multiple clients. This thinking needs to go into designing your form.

Not all attributes are equal. Some things you look at just because that is what a business owner wants, or it is important to your company. However there are some attributes that, if wrong, have a really big impact on your customer satisfaction results. Remember - we are supposed to be looking for what matters most to the customer—which means if an error is made on something that we know will impact on satisfaction, it is a really big deal. These are Critical to Quality as they will directly impact on the customer dissatisfaction e.g.

- Giving the wrong answer is unforgivable by the customer
- Being ultra-friendly and polite will not affect the customers opinion if they get the wrong answer
- Being of average friendliness will not even be noted in the survey if they get the right answer

- If you go above and beyond (calling back sooner, taking an extra step that was not asked for) Customer satisfaction will be very high

So your scoring needs to reflect the difference between CTQ attributes and soft skills (fluffy stuff) attributes. With the attributes defined, next you must work out how you will score them. By measuring you can compare individuals, teams and see performance improvement over time There are two schools of thought on scoring:

- Broad : A score from 1-5 or 1-10 that allows a broad scale of performance
- Simple: Bad, Good, Excellent or even Yes and No

The following table shows the relative merits of each approach.

Approach	Plus	Minus
Simple	a. Easier to be objective b. Easier to score factual attributes (it was done or not) c. Easier to train up all involved d. Easier to calibrate amongst those monitoring	a. Hard to score the softer skills because of limited range b. Does not leave much room for scoring "above and beyond" performance
Broad	a. Allows for scoring in a range rather than just yes or no b. Can be easier to calibrate with customer satisfaction because the scales match up more	a. Too much room for individual opinion b. May mean that the "big deal" attributes not always scored accurately
For Both	a. Big deal errors are those that are Critical To Quality., An error in a CTQ element should fail that monitoring transaction, irrespective of the scores given elsewhere. b. You need to pull out the results of the CTQ errors and consider them in a different way to the soft skills errors as actions are often different.	

In reality, few organisations have any level of rigour in their monitoring approach. Actually, the monitoring process has a mini-maturity model all of its own.

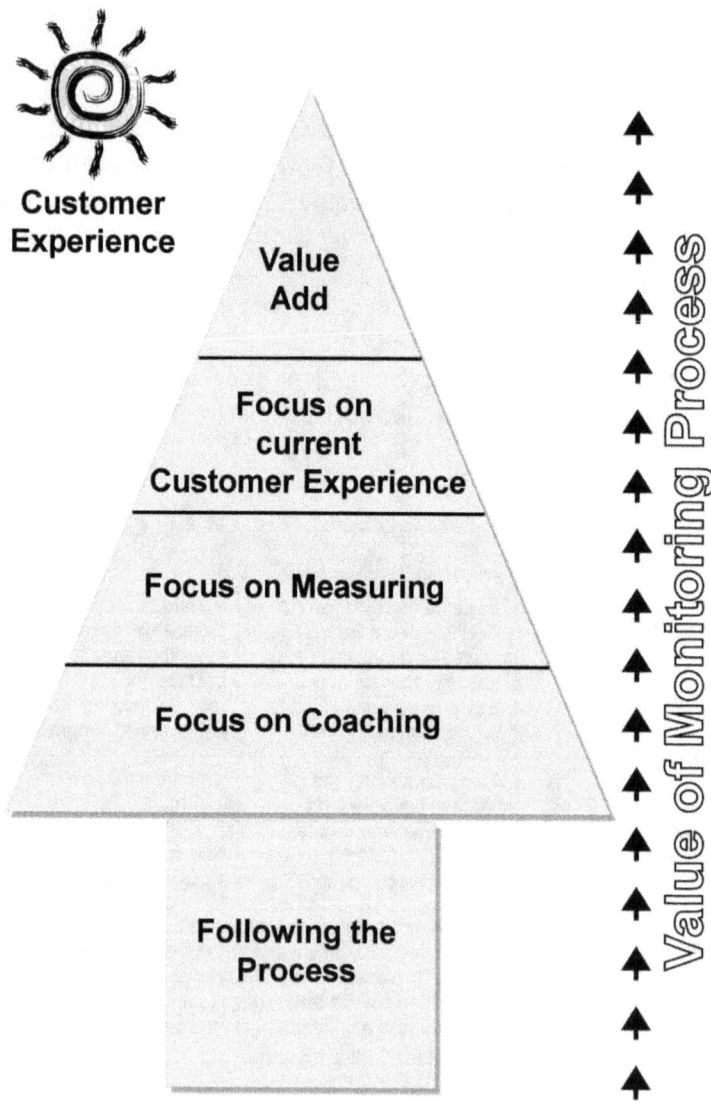

Figure 50. The Mini Monitoring Maturity Model

Getting to the top of the tree is not easy. It will mean that you are using the monitoring process to coach and develop individuals, to extract process level issues by looking at recurring issues from the scoring. Finally it requires that you look into your monitoring results to identify opportunities to enhance the customer experience and return that value add back to the business owner. This is a long way from "just getting it done".

The role of Customer Satisfaction Surveys

It is important to remember that at the point at which we get the results of a customer satisfaction survey, it is already too late. Surveys measure the opinion of the survey recipient based on an experience they have already had. This means that if the results are overly negative, then those customers, clients or staff may already be lost. The survey is a tool to improve the way your business operates in the future—a way to truly understand what is going on, and a way to prevent future issues. All the subjects we have covered in the chapter prior to this are direct prevention options; they prevent a problem from ever occurring. The survey is a fixer option; it helps us fix problems that already exist!

This means that satisfaction surveys are extremely valuable to prevent long-term damage through poor performance, but do not stand on their own, and prove most valuable when the results are fed into the preventive processes, such as recruiting and monitoring, to make them more robust.

There is a trick to getting this right. Most of us work on "gut instinct" to understand what is going on. However, as with everything we have looked at, we need to measure the data to truly understand it. I often find that gut instinct is not correct when it comes to customer satisfaction surveys. You can't beat just asking someone to get a true reflection of what they feel!

Our goal with customers is to answer their questions as quickly as we can, and on the first contact, if possible. We want to ensure that they leave the call with a good impression of the business owner because that means there is a higher likelihood that they will:

- Remain a loyal customer;
- Continue to use this product; and
- Recommend the business owner to friends and family if asked.

If we go "above and beyond the call of duty," we hope that the customer will be motivated to share their experience with friends and family even if they have not been asked, and potentially reflect this enthusiasm back to the business owner.

This behaviour is characteristic of customer loyalty, and this is what adds value to the business owner. This means that when conducting our customer satisfaction surveys, it is critical that we choose our questions carefully in order to get us the most accurate reflection of the impact we had on their opinion. In an article for the *Harvard Business Review,* Frederick F. Reichheld talks about "the one number you need to grow." He has conducted studies linking the different questions in satisfaction surveys and their relationship to true customer loyalty as measured by customer retention and re-purchase. By doing this correlation analysis, he determines that the most effective question across industry that measures customer loyalty is:

"How likely is it that you would recommend [company X] to a friend or colleague?"

I have been involved in many surveys. Most of the surveys I review have this question somewhere on them. However, when the management team sits down to review performance (if they do this), this question does not usually get even a second glance—the main focus is on the overall satisfaction. So what do we need in our surveys? In the contact centre industry there are some critical elements that should be included:

1. **You need to ensure that the question is based on the performance of your centre as opposed to the performance of the overall business owner's product or company.** For example, if the customer has to pay for the phone call at a premium rate then they are unlikely to be satisfied overall no matter how well you do your job. You need to ensure that you minimise the impact of this on the overall satisfaction result.

2. **You need a view over time, and you need this view to be appropriate to the rate of change.** For example, if you have high attrition and a rapidly changing product line, then you need to survey at a minimum monthly to enable you to spot trends in customer satisfaction and act on them before you lose too many customers. On the other hand, if it is a relatively stable environment, both in your own centre and in your product line, then every quarter or even every 6 months will give you a good reflection.

3. **You need to have enough information in the survey to analyse the overall results.** This means that if customer satisfaction drops you can look to other questions for the first clue about where the problem lies.

4. **You need to review both positive and negative results of a question.** As seen earlier, it is possible for both satisfaction and dissatisfaction to increase at the same time. A dissatisfied customer is likely to become a direct loss of revenue to the business owner—so this is critical.

5. **You need to make sure your sample is large enough and well distributed.** Your sample should be taken with some statistical validity. I have been

lucky enough to experiment with survey volumes, and I generally found that if we were trying to conduct an analysis based on less than 30 surveys, it was likely that one or two customers would skew the overall results, giving you erratic data. You must base your analysis on a reasonable sample size and on a reasonable spread over time and customer base.

Okay, now we have looked at the rules that should be followed, let me give you an example of a very simple survey. This is just an example of the questions, not the overall script.

Example Customer Satisfaction Survey

Question 1: How would you rate your overall satisfaction with the way the agent handled your enquiry?
1. Very Satisfied
2. Somewhat Satisfied
3. Somewhat Dissatisfied
4. Very Dissatisfied

Question 2: How would you rate your overall satisfaction with the service you received?
1. Very Satisfied
2. Somewhat Satisfied
3. Somewhat Dissatisfied
4. Very Dissatisfied

Question 3: How would you rate your overall satisfaction with the courteousness and friendliness with which your enquiry was handled?
1. Very Satisfied
2. Somewhat Satisfied
3. Somewhat Dissatisfied
4. Very Dissatisfied

Question 4: How satisfied are you that your enquiry was fully understood by the agent that handled it?
1. Very Satisfied
2. Somewhat Satisfied
3. Somewhat Dissatisfied
4. Very Dissatisfied

Question 5: How satisfied are you with the level of knowledge displayed by the agent who handled your enquiry?
1. Very Satisfied
2. Somewhat Satisfied
3. Somewhat Dissatisfied
4. Very Dissatisfied

Question 6: How satisfied are with the level of ownership taken by the agent who handled your enquiry?
1. Very Satisfied
2. Somewhat Satisfied
3. Somewhat Dissatisfied
4. Very Dissatisfied

Question 7: How satisfied are you that your original enquiry was answered and resolved?
1. Very Satisfied
2. Somewhat Satisfied
3. Somewhat Dissatisfied
4. Very Dissatisfied

Question 8: How satisfied are with speed with which you were able to reach someone to handle your enquiry?
1. Very Satisfied
2. Somewhat Satisfied
3. Somewhat Dissatisfied
4. Very Dissatisfied

Question 9: How satisfied are overall time it took to reach a final resolution on your enquiry?
1. Very Satisfied
2. Somewhat Satisfied
3. Somewhat Dissatisfied
4. Very Dissatisfied

Question 10: Based on the contact we are discussing, how has your opinion of [company X] changed?
1. It has improved
2. It has not changed
3. It has worsened

This is a very basic set of questions—and you should allow for the capturing of comments with each question, as this will help analysis. Questions 1 and 2 allow you to help the customer distinguish between the service you offer and that offered by the business owner. There may be little difference if your partnership with the business owner means that they have listened to your feedback over time and eliminated those areas that cause annoyance to customers. However, it is more likely that there will be a gap in these results. When looking at the results of these questions you should ensure that you split the satisfaction and dissatisfaction results and analyse them separately.

Questions 3-9 then allow you to gather enough data to analyse the results of the first 2 questions by looking at the levels of satisfaction within specific areas. It helps to ask two "speed" questions. At first glance it may seem a waste of time to ask if the customer was happy with the "speed of answer" (Question 8) when you know you have switch data to show this. In reality you are correct. What you really want to know is how satisfied they are with the overall resolution time (Question 9). This is the question that gives an accuracy reflection. However, asking both questions helps the customer to understand the difference in what you are asking for—allowing for a more reflective answer to Question 9!

Scoring Scale

Having worked out your questions, the next step is to establish the scale for scoring. Everyone has their own opinion on the best scale. The following factors should be considered when looking at the appropriate scale to use.

1.   Comparative data: Once you have your results, you need some form of context to understand how good or bad they are. This usually comes from within the industry but given that the business owner almost definitely has a product that is not contact centre

based, then it is worth crossing industries to establish your benchmarks. When looking at comparative data, the scale used is critical. Take the following statement: *"80% of our customers say they are satisfied with our service."* It is very hard for us to benchmark if this is good if we don't know how it is measured. Is this a 5-point scale from "very satisfied" to "very dissatisfied"? Is there a neutral option? How is this counted? In order to draw conclusions on where you stand you need to be sure you are comparing apples with apples.

2. Shorter scale or longer scale: Some people prefer to give the fewest number of options possible—maybe a 4-point scale ("very satisfied," "satisfied," "dissatisfied,," and "very dissatisfied"). This is easier to remember but may force someone to choose an option that does not quite fit. This can be either or a good or a bad thing! A longer scale ("extremely satisfied," "very satisfied," "somewhat satisfied," "neither satisfied nor dissatisfied," "somewhat dissatisfied," "very dissatisfied," and "extremely dissatisfied") gives more of a range of options, meaning that the customer can more accurately reflect their experience. The down side is the top ends of the scale may never get a score, depending on the culture. For a British customer to state they are "extremely satisfied" is a real rarity! (Although maybe "extremely dissatisfied" is a little more likely....)

3. Neutral: You also need to decide if you are willing to have a neutral point in your scale. A neutral point (neither satisfied nor dissatisfied) gives the customer the option to not be swayed in either direction—to basically not commit to a feeling about the experience. You then need to decide how you will factor that into the scoring. You may decide that if you have not had a strong enough impact on the customer, then it should

count as a miss and you take no credit for it in the scoring. You may also decide that if they were unhappy with the experience they would say something and count it as a hit. Or you may even discount it altogether—however, this option means you are missing out on data you have gathered from customers, so it is a real missed opportunity. Personally, I would not include a neutral option, and thus get rid of any doubt. Unfortunately, most common benchmarking data is based on ticks in the top 2 boxes ("very satisfied" and "satisfied") on a 5-point scale, so it includes a neutral.

Obviously, once you have chosen your scale you need to stick to it, so you can at least get a feel for the trend in the data.

Delivery Method

Right, we have our questions and our scale worked out, and we know how big the sample size should be. How do we now actually conduct the surveys? There are various approaches to conducting surveys. The simplest approach is to get someone else to do it for you! In the same way as you are experts at handling contacts, these companies are experts at surveying and correlating the responses. The down side of this approach is that it can prove quite expensive, as you pay per survey and the price includes the resources to build, deliver and analyse the survey. The positive is that you get an objective and balanced report which saves your key staff time and eliminates doubts from the mind of the business owner that you may have "adjusted" the results in some way.

Irrespective of whether you choose to use an external party or conduct the surveys yourself, there are essentially three different delivery methods to consider:

Method	Description	Advantages	Disadvantages
Phone	This is the traditional approach of calling the customer and recording their responses. It requires a sample to be produced from the case logging tool and the list then needs working through in some random order.	a. You can clarify anything the customer says. b. The success rate is probably the highest of all the methods - so you will get the most successful responses	a. It requires you capture the customers phone number on the contact b. It requires a resource to make the phone calls c. The time of day is critical to the success rate d. It can be regarded as less objective e. It can annoy the customers to be called f. If there have been multiple contacts it can be hard to make sure the survey is based on the one you controlled. g. You need to do a data extract
E-Mail	There are a couple of options here. One is to attach a link or the survey to an email response automatically. The other is to extract the email addresses and do a mail drop to all in one go	a. Survey can be sent on every contact. b. Responses are ongoing so you don't need to wait for end of month or quarter for trends c. Cheapest option in terms of delivery because it does not require a resource d. No issues with sample objectivity if sent to every customer	a. Security risk if a file is attached b. You need to have a way of stopping the customer responding multiple times. c. Requires email address d. Response rate not as good as phone
IVR	With an IVR survey a customer will be given the option to complete a survey after a call, at which point they get put into an IVR and are asked a set of questions	Does not require any details to be taken from the customer. This is the only option when this is the case	a. This can be the most expensive option b. You need to be careful to make it objective - agents should not be able to choose which customers to put through c. Often criticized for capturing input from only the most dissatisfied customers d. Often requires good speech recognition engine if you want to capture comments. e. Agents must be trained to hang up on the customers.

Figure 55. Relative merits of different survey methods

When designing your approach, you will need to consider the advantages and disadvantages of each method and work out which ones are most important to your organisation. Remember, if you are in an outsource environment, it is possible that you may choose the cheapest option as part of your standard value add, but charge some part back to the business owner if you choose to take on one of the more comprehensive options.

Summary

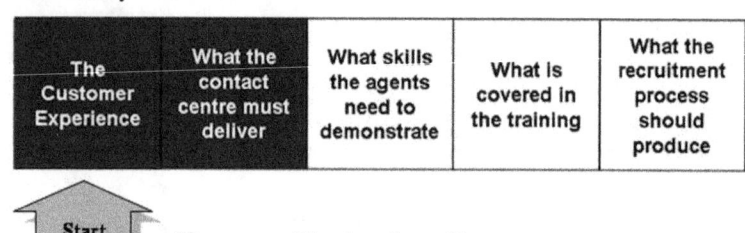

The Customer Experience	What the contact centre must deliver	What skills the agents need to demonstrate	What is covered in the training	What the recruitment process should produce

Figure 25: Top level quality process

Throughout this chapter we have looked at quality in a kind of "back to front" approach. We start by looking at the customer experience we are aiming for, and everything else is geared up to help us achieve it. This is the highest point on the maturity tree because it is a proactive approach to managing the business and provides an opportunity to truly add value back to the business owner.

Without this, it is possible to operate. However, to achieve true efficiency requires continuous monitoring and an approach to improvement that is driven, not by your business owner, but by your own organisation.

Surely this costs money, though? Is it not the case that high quality equals high cost? Categorically no! It is actually the opposite. Let's look at some of the costs involved in getting it wrong.

Figure 32: What does it cost to get it wrong?

In reality, the cost of getting it wrong is something most organisations can't afford

Final Chapter

The Future

Dealing with what you have

This all sounds great so far (or I hope it does), but in reality we are generally already in a situation where we have established our contact centre—we are already handling contacts from customers day in and day out. We are certainly not in a position to get rid of all our staff, redefine the skill sets, and re-recruit based on a defined customer experience. So is all hope lost for us?

Well the good news is that there is still room to move here! Whilst you can't change your recruitment criteria for existing staff, you can define it for all new recruits. You can also spend some time defining what the customers really want. This is a lot easier to do once the business is live—because not only do you have various points of data that you can review around call drivers, you can also go right ahead and ask the customers what matters most to them.

Using this "voice of the customer" measure, you are then in a position to identify the true Value Add elements of the service you deliver and apply this knowledge to your existing processes to eliminate, as much as possible, the non-Value Add elements.

This can be created for an existing customer base. It does, however, require the establishment of two of the classic contact centre quality measurements: first, the customer satisfaction survey, and second, the approach taken to monitoring the contact quality.

Steps to establish control in an existing operation

The following details the steps you need to look at in an existing operation to allow your organisation to move up to the top of the maturity tree.

1. Define the skill requirements for each role that interacts with the customer.
2. Update your recruitment process to ensure that you either
   a. Recruit people with the necessary aptitude to gain the skills; or
   b. Have enough training to fill the gap between the point at which they are recruited and the point that you let them interact with your customers.
3. Introduce a "value" into the management team of your organisation to ensure that no one gets to deal with customers until you are sure they are ready—you will not risk losing customers for the sake of "warm bodies on seats."
4. Measure all the things that we have identified in earlier chapters to establish business performance Use this to work out where your current problems lie.
5. Survey your customers and the business owners—see what they really think! Use this to look at the way you recruit, train and manage.
6. Work out how you are going to bring your existing staff base up to the level you want by focussing on

- a. Communication of the information they need to handle the customers;
- b. Verifying through some form of testing process that this is understood; and
- c. Monitoring the calls for quality and accurate use of the information you have provided.
7. Build a management information framework to clearly identify what information you expect each level of your organisation to look at and what information you expect them to act on. Work out who will communicate with the business owner, how often and what you would define as "success" for this relationship.

Remember, making lots of money from a business owner might be nice for your business, but it puts the contract at risk in the long term if you are not delivering value for the price. It exposes you to another provider coming along with a lower-cost option for the same operational targets.

Driving the change

So what happens when they just don't get it? Here we are, talking about a bunch of very high level concepts. Assuming that as you read this book, you realise that this is exactly what you need—do you now have everything to get this in place in your organisation?

Unfortunately, it is not that simple. It never is!

The problem with a concept is that it is too high level. To get a concept adopted, you must somehow tap into the "What's in it for me?" factor at every level of your organisation. I used to have an American manager who said we should tune in to radio station "WIIFM." It's corny, but this is the question everyone asks, along with "So what?" and "Why should I?"

Actually, this is nothing more than basic change management. To operate an efficient and effective operation it is not enough to know what you must do, you must also consider the best approach to driving your organisation through change. A lot comes back to the concepts of "vision" discussed in the second chapter.

Jack Welch uses the approach in Figure 33 to describe the changes driven by implementing Six Sigma:

Figure 33: The approach to change management described by Jack Welch

I am not going to cover all the different approaches to change management, although I do suggest you start with the classic book, *Who Moved My Cheese?* by Spencer Johnson. That said, I do suggest that you become familiar with some quality frameworks, because it really helps to have a distinct structure to follow when improving. The next step will then be to audit your organisation, either with an internal team or using an external company to gain credibility and to keep the organisation focussed on a goal. It is a great organisation that is able to drive this scale of change with nothing but its own internal deadlines.

It is more likely that you will need the additional drive provided by an external "certification" date.

You will also be able to get some decent marketing out of one of the external bodies so that you can use the approach not just for organisational improvement, but also to blow away your competition when it comes to winning new business. I have seen businesses advertising on the television using the accessibility and helpfulness of their Contact centre as a key selling point. I think in the past, everyone used to hide the fact that they had a contact centre because the public did not like the idea of the "impersonal" approach. These days, it is accepted. Many people have dealt with or worked in a contact centre (admittedly, not always a good experience!), which has opened it up as a unique selling point when marketed correctly. This is particularly relevant with the widespread use of the offshore marketplace as a cost reduction choice—the industry is now beginning to see what was taken for granted on-shore!

The role of Quality Frameworks

There are many quality frameworks that have been developed over the years. The challenge in finding the right one for our industry is that they are mostly designed for dealing with concrete processes. Manufacturing is one of the longest lived and best established industries going. As a result they have developed a number of quality approaches focussed on process control and process improvement. The term "defective parts per million" comes from manufacturing. Think about this term for a second. It means that they aspire to such a high level of accuracy that they count mistakes out of 1 million. Now look at how that would apply to the contact centre—defective calls per million? Defective answers per million opportunities? How would you even start measuring this?

The reality is that because we are dealing with the invisible, it is nearly impossible to check every contact, especially calls. It is also impossible to check after a call has been taken—because it has disappeared. If a part in manufacturing is defective, it will be around to examine and look at improving. You can look at issues like "wastage"—materials cast out from the manufacturing process after a product is produced. In the contact centre, the closest we have is an abandoned call—once more, an invisible item.

So this means we can learn from manufacturing in terms of how we look at processes and map them, but we can't take a manufacturing quality framework and assume it is of any value to our industry.

Where does this leave us? Well, many organisations that have contact centres also have a main line of business that the contact centre serves—maybe it is a supermarket or a computer manufacturer. These products usually fall into the right industry for some form of quality framework—usually ISO-9001. What then happens is that the main part of the business insists on the contact centre meeting this same standard. It is usually not a very good fit, and whilst they get the certificate, it does little for effective contact centre operations. To understand why this does not quite work, let's look at some of the applicable quality frameworks with a brief summary—this is by no means an exhaustive list—to get a thorough comparison on some of the different standards you should read "Assessing Business Excellence" by L. J. Porter, S. J. Tanner

Here, I am focussing on those that I feel are either perfectly matched to this industry, or are already in widespread use in the industry. It is by no means an exhaustive list, but it does highlight some of the different options that are available.

ISO	This is a widely used standard with a strong focus on process adherence. It is possible to use ISO to good effect, but more often the use of ISO is not geared up to achieve the highest benefit. Organisations often put on a big push to get their certification the first time, and then maintain it through smaller annual visits. The focus in these cases is generally on clear documented processes. It is possible for performance to be poor, but still achieve certification. I have seen ISO used well to drive organisational consistency, but more often I have seen it as purely a certificate. It seems such a shame to only use it for this - it requires so much time and effort to implement, you really want to make sure you get the return on it
COPC®	Unlike the others in the realm, this standard was written for the contact centre environment - as such it is a little more tailored to drive performance than other standards. In fact, reading the standard is almost like a handbook on how to run a contact centre. Its focus is on performance first and process second. It requires a high level of commitment from the organisation to make it work as it impacts on every aspect of the contact centre business, but as it focuses on performance the results are there to be gained if used correctly.
LEAN	Like Six Sigma, this is less a certification and more an approach. It fits in to the previous two standard frameworks (as opposed to replacing them). The approach used by Lean is to break down the complexity of the processes, identifying the non-value add elements and thus speeding up the process. When used with Six Sigma, it can be a very powerful approach to process reengineering
Six Sigma	As with Lean, this is an approach to process reengineering that ties in with some of the standard quality frameworks out there. The focus of six sigma is to remove defects in a process. Originally applied in a manufacturing environment, this is being successfully implemented across other industries and is particularly popular in the contact centre environment at the moment.

While some of these standards have a certification association, it is a dangerous path to choose to aim for "the badge" as opposed to the improvement it will help your business achieve. Of course, a nice shiny certificate is great—you can show it off to your friends, hang it in the reception area of your building, put it in presentations to the client, etc. However, if this is all you do, then you are wasting the money you have spent implementing it (and it is not usually an insignificant amount!). All these approaches can help you climb the maturity tree for your organisation, reducing costs and adding value at the same time. This is the true benefit. If you are going to push to certification, use it as a means of giving your organisation a way of measuring achievement to goals, an excuse to celebrate, and a physical indication of some of the less tangible things they have managed to achieve.

If you have multiple locations in your contact centre organisation, you should give serious thought to developing your own standardised company approach. After all, wherever the business owner puts the business, they should expect to receive the same standard of service delivery. If you use any of the above approaches, or any of the alternatives out there, it is possible to have a very different look and feel to the way each of your contact centre locations work. Short-term this may work, but it is not a good strategy for long-term growth. My suggestion is that you roll out one of the industry standard approaches and focus on getting that in place in every location first—and then build on that to define your own way of working, a kind of template that can apply to any location you currently have and any location you may open in the future. This will be particularly useful if you're considering an offshore or near-shore location.

The role of auditing—the best laid plans of mice and men...

So, how do you find out what is really going on in your organisation?

When I visit an organisation, I sit down with staff and observe what they do. I watch agents taking calls and processing emails; I chat to management about how their team or their piece of business is performing. At the end of a few days of doing this, I have a pretty clear picture of how things really are in a particular location.

Then I do a report to the management team, and so often what I hear is, "You have to trust your people"; and "They understand that the customer is important and they will do their best for them." Whilst these statements may make you feel all warm and fuzzy inside, the reality of what we see is often very different from the management perception. I also find that those who have not been through the experience of being audited themselves question every detail of a report such as this—because it is often misaligned with their view of the world, and they have no basis for establishing the credibility of what you are telling them. Those who have experienced the audit themselves rarely question the findings. They can see how the information is generated and understand the opportunities they were given to explain their operations.

The reality is that we all look at the world differently. These different views are brought together in a working environment, and we have to come to agreement on driving forward and managing business. However, if I would ask each of you to describe the cover of this book, you would approach it in different ways. These different approaches should be multiplied by the number of people in your organisation and can result in as many different ways of doing things as you have people! Let's be honest—just because a process has been written, this does not guarantee the way that process will be executed.

What you need is some mechanism to ensure that the blueprints for how you want your organisation to run are actually followed. Some things can be measured by satisfaction surveys—staff, customer or client. It is far easier to get it right first time than it is to fix something that has been incorrectly implemented (that is, assuming you even notice that it was not implemented as you had expected). Once more, we are talking here about fire prevention instead of fire fighting. Resource is often quoted as the reason for not getting on top of this stuff—but don't forget to ask yourself, "If you haven't got time to do a good enough job and get it right the first time, how will you possibly have time to do it all over again when it doesn't work?"

I have not found anything that is more effective for building a picture of everything that goes on in an organisation than auditing.

So what is an audit? When most of us have encountered the word "audit," it is in a financial context—an audit trail. It is a word that has quite negative connotations. In the context of this book, an audit it is merely an honest observational examination of the execution of the processes in your business.

It is an open process, where everyone involved in the process is kept fully informed of the findings of the process as you go through it. To conduct this sort of audit uses quite a different approach from other types of audits. The goal is multi-fold:

- To observe a process in action, allowing you to see if the process is being consistently executed and if the design of the process is workable within the organisation;
- To look for opportunities for improvement;
- To get direct feedback on what sort of environment/culture your company is providing for people to work in;
- To validate the source and calculation of the key metrics that you use in managing your business; and
- To see if what you think is in place really is what is happening.

There are many different ways you can resource this audit approach. One way is to establish an overall quality group that defines the process, and then allocate a certain amount of time each month that each of your senior managers will give over to actually conducting an audit. Managers should always conduct audits of units other than their own, if possible. This allows them to remain objective, and it has the added benefit of giving them a chance to see another way of operating that they can learn from.

Another approach is to have some form of quality representative allocated to each business unit. The representative would be responsible for auditing but also for other quality duties, such as contact quality monitoring, customer satisfaction surveys, data reporting, etc.

Lastly you may consider a combination of the approaches — a quality representative who works with a number of volunteers within the organisation who conduct auditing of other teams. This allows the volunteers to become more involved in, and take more ownership of, the improvement efforts in the organisation.

Auditing is a mainstay of what I do. I find it the only way to truly find out what is going on in an organisation. It saves hours of those painful discussions in the boardroom or senior management meetings, where a bunch of managers sit around with some data, struggling to make sense of it and jumping to conclusions about what caused the results. Good auditing data will fit into this picture with clear facts, based on observation, which are impossible to refute.

If you decide that you want to implement an audit process — here are some general guidelines that you should follow in order to make it as effective as possible:

Stuff to think about when auditing

Define the framework that you are planning to follow for the audit.
- This might be one of the existing frameworks out there.
- You might choose to use the maturity model from this book.
- You may want to design your own approach based on how you really want your organisation to work.

Identify who will do the audits.
- Will you use a dedicated quality person?
- Will you allow management in the organisation to audit each other?
- Will you have a combination of quality people and operational team members?

Identify how often you will audit.
- Audit often enough to create visibility of the effectiveness of changes.
- Don't audit too often. This will leave you without the time to take sufficient action.

- Depending on the pace of change in your organisation, every 6 months is generally an appropriate frequency.

Identify how the results will be reported and who will see the report.

- There is no point looking at it if you don't do something with what you see.
- You should always report out to those people who have been audited.
- Management will need some sort of view.
- Results should always be factual—avoid judgements as people respond defensively. Remember, you are not auditing to police the process—you are auditing to improve it.

Train up the right people to audit.

- This is not an interrogation—people need to learn how to ask questions. It is not something that comes naturally to everyone.
- Train them on how to ask questions, how to interpret the answers and how to communicate the results.

Through auditing I have seen many things, including:

- Processes that occurred which management insisted did not occur; e.g., agents making callbacks to customers;
- Systems problems that were limiting the agents' ability to do their jobs;
- New agents who had no idea where to find answers so were asking other new agents;
- High variation in handle times because of slow typing speed despite the manager insisting that someone was their best agent; and
- "Good agents" mentoring new agents, and then, when you sit with the good agents, you realise they are not that good after all.

Remember in Chapter 5 I talked about the problems we had with our Callback process? It was the auditing process that allowed us to get to the bottom of that one. The list is endless, to be honest—but you should get my point by now. Auditing is a great tool.

How do Offshore, Near Shore, and Onshore all fit in?

No matter how well your own operation is working, there is still the opportunity to save costs by putting your business in a location that has a cheaper labour market.

In this book, we have talked a lot about how to achieve the balance of adding value to the customer, without adding cost to your business. This is where the option of putting your business offshore becomes very appealing. If approximately 80% of the costs in your business relate to the salaries you pay your staff, then what easier way could there be to save money than to cut those salaries by 80%? In the Indian offshore market, the annual salary of an agent can work out to be the same as the monthly salary of a UK agent.

With this in mind, and the main cost of business being your people, why would you not automatically send all your business offshore? India, Egypt, South Africa and the Philippines all have a high percentage of their population who speak English and are well-educated. There are also the offshore locations for other languages—Morocco and Egypt are good for French, South Africa works for Dutch, Poland for German.

It's interesting that in the UK, we have started seeing adverts with companies advertising an onshore, local contact centre as a unique selling point. What changed in the world that resulted in your contact centre being a key part of your sales pitch? Surely it is supposed to be all about the product?

So it is a good idea from a cost perspective to move our business offshore...or is it? Certainly the salary costs are lower but there are other direct and indirect costs that come into play when you move into an offshore market.

The direct (and usually un-budgeted) cost is that of the support necessary to enable the offshore operation to function effectively. In order to benefit from a reduced labour cost, you must establish your business in a less developed country. This means that the management knowledge has also not yet been developed, and that there will be little experience of what it takes to set up a contact centre operation. End result? Planes full of your experienced managers backwards and forwards all the time. Without this the business never gets on its feet and you find your onshore location flooded with client and customer complaints and customer issues.

As you send these people out there, not only do you incur massive costs, you also leave your onshore operations exposed. In one of the companies I worked for, when we launched our Indian operations, our travel budget in the first 6 months ended up £1 million over budget. This is a pretty direct cost of doing offshore business and is quite a common side effect for companies to experience.

Indirect costs relate to your customer experience. We know there is no such thing as a free lunch! You have to accept that because you are putting your business in a remote, under-developed location, there will be an impact on your customer satisfaction. The question is—how much are you willing to risk for the sake of the cost savings? You often hear companies referring to putting their "low value" business out there. Who can afford to define the loss of even one customer as acceptable in today's competitive marketplace? When looking at our maturity model, we are miles away from Value Add in choosing an offshore strategy. It is never a decision based on quality; it is purely based on costs.

This means that when you consider putting your business offshore, you need to also consider the following:

1. What level of customer satisfaction will be acceptable?

It is going to be lower than your normal level, but how much lower is okay? You may also find you need to rephrase your customer satisfaction survey questions to meet an offshore environment. The common question "Did the agent understand your enquiry" is too ambiguous, as understanding may relate to either a physical language issue (you could not make out each other's words) or a situation where the words were clear, but it was the meaning that was not understood. I would also suggest a question on empathy that you pay particular attention to. This is a common problem with the Indian contact centre operations and one that causes significant levels of customer frustration.

You should be particularly focussed on any customer feedback you can get hold of. You should be sampling at a frequency to analyse this weekly and have someone responsible for trawling through it with a fine-tooth comb for any indication of a problem. Set a clear threshold of what is acceptable. 85% when you are used to 90% is not a big deal. 75% when you are used to 80% is. Look for other indications, too, like a reduction in first contact volume and a reduction in first contact resolution. Watch out for just looking at volumes—if the offshore location is doing a bad job of answering questions, volumes will become unnaturally inflated by repeat calls. It is the first contact resolution that you should really focus on.

Also, do not just focus on satisfaction—the first indication of a problem may be in the dissatisfaction results. So that should be the first number you dig into. Think of other measures you have of customer satisfaction—maybe cancellations of a service, repeat purchase volume or something else that you can look at. If you accept that any of these metrics can suffer because it is worth it for the cost saving—be very clear on how much is acceptable.

2. What additional costs are you expecting (and willing) to incur?

You have to accept that there will be costs to your onshore business of going offshore. It is not all about cost savings. It will take between one and two years to realise the true cost savings of an offshore location—depending on the location you are going to and the scale of the offshoring.

First look at the management in the location you are going to. Many companies choose to partner with an organisation that already exists in a country. This means that you can assess their current level of management skills and work out how much support you will need to give. Will you be sending out supervisors, Call centre managers, or both? How long will they need to be there? Will you send management from support functions such as HR, to teach them how to recruit and train? Do not think you can get away with remote support on this stuff. My experience is that someone needs to be there—otherwise you may be told things are getting done that are in fact going nowhere.

Once you have worked out the level of support you will need to provide, you need to start planning the costs. This starts with flights—often business class, especially if you do not give enough notice. Once a venue becomes popular as an offshore location, the flights start to sell out very quickly. Next you need to think of accommodation. There is too much risk to leave this to chance. We are talking underdeveloped countries, after all, and you may expect the accommodation to be offered at the same kind of low rates as the labour, but this is not the case. Hotels in key offshore locations begin to sell out very quickly, and they soon realise they can charge premium rates and still get business. This has particularly been the case in India. This means that a better alternative will probably be an apartment— but these will also end up at a premium as an area becomes more popular. After that you have living costs, and, if you ask someone to stay there a while, flights for family and flights home for them. As they are there on your business, everything they do is a living cost that can be charged back to you. By now you should be starting to understand where I am coming from—there are some real, direct overhead costs of doing business offshore that you must budget for so that you can still make a margin that you expected. Obviously, the longer you continue to offshore the less these costs become. The question is, can you sustain this early additional cost and will you survive the upset to the customers and the business owners of the move long enough to truly see the benefits?

I have a theory that the best way to choose a "perfect match" in an offshore location is to go and hang out there as a customer—in coffee shops, restaurants, retail stores. When in these public environments, make jokes, subtle ones. Say things that are humorous that people would normally laugh at. Try sarcasm and other more subtle forms of humour. If they laugh, then you have a good choice of an offshore location. It means they are in tune to your culture. If they do not, then I predict you will have a problem. This, I have found, is the significant difference between India and Egypt as an offshore location. In Egypt they laugh at the right times, and read you well when you are getting frustrated or annoyed. I did not find this the case in India. Bear in mind, however, that all this applies to the UK sense of humour (which we all know is unique). For each country where you are looking to offshore, you need to try this test.

When considering any offshore location, the important thing to remember is that irrespective of where your contact centre is physically based, you are still dealing with the same customers. Any degradation of quality should be a deliberate decision based on an understanding of what you currently do. If you do not have your own local operations in order, it is highly unlikely that offshoring the business will make you any more successful. The short-term financial gain will be cancelled out by longer-term reduction in customer retention.

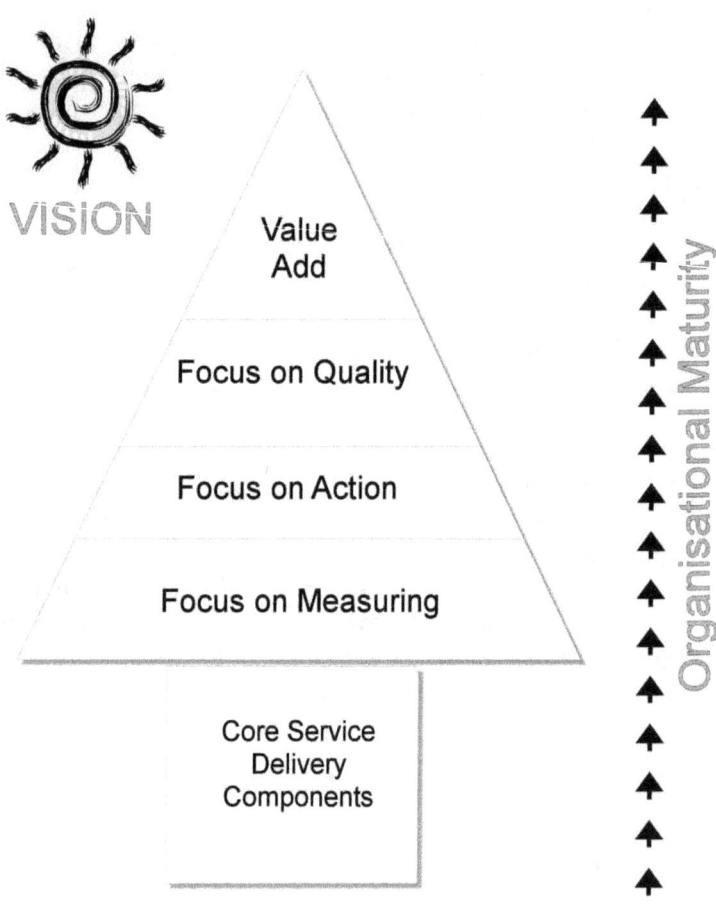

Figure 5 : The Maturity Tree

The Maturity Model - Revisited - A Mature view of the value of a call and its value

So how does this "mature" contact centre look and feel? It is hard to say exactly, because I have not found an organisation that has achieved this yet. However, let me try and paint a picture for you of what would happen in contact centre utopia.

First, from the people point of view—you have a really rigorous recruitment process that means that you have people with the right skills dealing with your customers. As you get constant, daily customer feedback from your surveying process, you are watching for changes in customer behaviour. You categorise these changes into two groups: process change and individually generated change. With process changes, you analyse and model the impact they will have on your business in the future. You also keep an open dialogue with the business owner so they have the same visibility of their customer as you do.

When you look at the individual level, you are trying to see how the way you have been managing the centre has been affecting the customer experience. This will involve reviewing the operational metrics such as service level by interval, volumes presented by interval and AHT by interval. Once you have established any causes at the operational level, you will focus on team and agent performance. Is there a particular team that has highly variable performance? How are the results of the contact quality monitoring tying into what your customers are telling you? Are handle time and adherence in control? You will be looking at this dashboard real time, and understand that if something happens in one afternoon to affect customer satisfaction—then you must be particularly vigilant on other days so that you don't damage more customers than necessary.

At the end of each week you will compare your forecasted revenue and margin with your actual. There will be no surprises here because you have been watching all the key metrics closely and already understand anything that will have been impacted.

On a monthly basis you can think about your strategy for the next 3 to 4 months. What are the seasonal trends you are expecting? What are the pros and cons of downsizing vs. keeping additional overhead on board because you know the volume will increase? What are the additional revenue opportunities with the business owner? Can you start up-selling or cross-selling and increase revenue per customer? Can you make the customer experience better by some form of call avoidance strategy?

At the end of the day, you will measure your success in the following ways:
- You have retained your existing client for many years.
- You have grown the revenue from your existing client year on year, whilst making your client feel like they are receiving good value for their money.
- Your profit is on track to forecast.
- Your staff measures show that you are doing as much as you can, and your attrition and absenteeism are both low compared to benchmarks.
- You have a reputation for consistent operational performance.
- You have happy customers.

This is not an easy list—that is why contact centre destruction is such an easy thing to achieve. However, just because it is not easy, does not mean that it is not possible!

What you have read in this book may sound like common sense. You may also have read it and felt it was familiar because you are doing parts of it already. However, if you are not doing all of it, then you are not moving up the maturity tree.

It is not enough to deliver excellence in quality but ignore the efficiencies.

It is not enough to go all out for service and speed on the assumption that you will achieve customer satisfaction that way.

It is not enough to tighten your belt and watch every efficiency metric but give less focus to the impact on speed and quality. Doing them all, at the same time—that is the real art of managing a contact centre

Appendix A

Sample Standard Contact Centre Metric Definitions

Metric	Definition	Possible Calculation
FTE	Full-time equivalent	(Total hours per day per person - paid breaks) * days of week.
Service Level E.g. 80% in 40 seconds	The percentage of transactions that are responded to in a specified timeframe (the timeframe is called the cycle time).	No. calls answered in cycle time / no. calls offered
Abandonment Rate E.g. <5%	Calls answered by the switch so they end up in the contact centre queue for handling, but the customer hangs up or drops off before you can answer	Calls abandoned / offered Calls Or Calls offered − calls answered / calls offered
Calls Offered	The total number of calls that are presented. NOTE: be aware if you are looking at calls presented to switch or to agent queue	
Calls Answered	The total number of calls presented to the skill that are answered by an agent	
Calls Abandoned	Calls answered by the switch so they end up in the contact centre queue for handling, but the customer hangs up or drops off before you can answer	
Average Handle Time (AHT)	The average amount of time an agent spends processing a transaction. This includes time spent talking with end users, putting end users on hold and wrapping up the transaction	(Total talk time + total hold time + total wrap) / total answered calls
Average Talk Time (ATT)	The average length of time an agent spends on the telephone with the end user. This should include hold time if this is not shown separately	Total talk time + total hold time / total answered calls
After Call Work (ACW)	The average amount of time an agent spends at the end of the call completing the transaction before they are available to take the next transaction	Total ACW time / total answered calls
Occupancy	Time that an agent spends on inbound calls as a % of the time that they are available to be on inbound calls. It excludes all Aux time.	(Talk + hold + wrap) / (talk + hold + wrap + available time)
Utilisation	Time that an agent spends on client activity as a % of the time that they are logged in.	(Talk + hold + wrap + productive aux) / logged in time
Monitorings Free From Critical Errors	A critical error is considered to be something which is detrimental to the call and would therefore fail the call immediately with one critical error	No. of monitorings free from critical errors / total monitoring sessions
Monitorings Free From Non-Critical Errors	A non-critical error is considered to be something which would cause an annoyance to the end user. Too many non-critical errors would therefore lead to a critical error	No of Monitorings Free from Non-Critical Errors / Total Monitoring Sessions
Overall Satisfaction	Of the customers contacted, what percentage are satisfied or very satisfied	(Total scoring Very Satisfied + Total scoring Satisfied) / Total responses
Overall Dissatisfaction	The number of customers who expressed any negative comment on the service provided.	Total scoring Very Dissatisfied/ Total responses
Absenteeism	What percentage of agents had an unauthorised or unscheduled absence?	Number of hours absent / total hours scheduled
Attrition	What is the overall percentage of attrition	Volume of leavers / Average monthly headcount

Appendix B

Financial Terms

Metric	Definition
Gross Fee Revenue	The total amount charged to the business owner on the invoice
Net Fee Revenue	What is left after accruals and pass through revenue has been taken out
Pass through	Usually things like setup costs, shipping and cost of phone calls that are charged to client at cost, hence pass through
Cost of Sales (COS)	How much it costs to get the revenue in
Direct	This is the direct salaries of those people actually generating the revenue - and these are people factored into the billing of the client. Usually agents, specialists and supervisors
Semi-Direct	These are specific costs you make for a client like those who manage supervisors, those who do training etc. They are often not paid for by the client.
Gross Margin	When you have taken your costs from your revenue, this is what is left.
P & L	Profit and Loss. This the sheet that puts all the numbers together
CAPEX (Capital Expenditure)	When you buy an item over a certain value it becomes an asset to the organization and then is subject to depreciation in value etc. The process of buying these items is Capital Expenditure

Appendix C

IQ Test Answers

Which number should come next in this series: 144, 121, 100, 81, 64, ?
a. 17
b. 19
c. 36
d. 49, this is 7*7, 64 is 8*8, 81 is 9*9 etc
e. 50

Julie likes 400 but not 300; 100 but not 99; 3600 but not 3700. Which does she like?
a. 900 this is 30*30, she likes numbers where the square root is a round number (20 is the square root of 400, 10 of 100, 60 of 3600)
b. 1000
c. 1100
d. 1200

In a race from point A to point B and back, Jim averages 30 miles per hour to point B and 10 miles per hour back to point A. Julie averages 20 miles per hour in both direction. Between Jim and Julie, who finished first?
a. Jim
b. Julie
c. They tie - the average speed is the same over the same total distance.
d. Neither
e. Impossible to tell

References

Collins, Jim; 2001; *From Good to Great*; HarperCollins

Marcus Buckingham and Curt Coffman;2000; *First Break all the Rules*; Simon&Schuster

O'Boyle, Tomas F.;1998;*At Any Cost*; Vintage Books

Shultz, Howard; 1997,*Pour your heart into it*; Hyperion

Slater, Robert; 1999; *Jack Welch and the GE Way*; McGraw Hill

George, Michael L. ; 2003; *Lean Six Sigma for Service*; McGraw Hill

Nelson, Bob; 1994;*1001 ways to Reward Employees*; Thomas Allen & Son

Johnson, Spence; 1999;*Who Moved My Cheese?* ;Vermillion

L. J. Porter and S. J. Tanner ; 2003; *Assessing Business Excellence*; Butterworth-Heinmann Ltd